RYAN WILSON

Ryan Wilson was born and grew up in Northern Ireland where he knew from an early age that he wanted to be a teacher. Straight out of university, he did a PGCE at the age of twenty-one and, after his training, spent five years teaching in a comprehensive school in Essex before leaving for a Head of Department job in London. He loved every aspect of teaching – the planning, the kids, the colleagues, the material, even the marking – but after a decade of budget cuts, hyper-accountability and unsupportive governments Ryan eventually left teaching to go back to university and now works as a radio producer and reporter. He has written about education for the *Guardian* and the *Times Educational Supplement*, including taking on the mantle of the *Guardian*'s Secret Teacher.

Follow Ryan on Twitter @rhwilson83

Let That Be a Lesson

A Teacher's Life in the Classroom

RYAN WILSON

VINTAGE

1 3 5 7 9 10 8 6 4 2

Vintage is part of the Penguin Random House group of companies
whose addresses can be found at global.penguinrandomhouse.com

Penguin
Random House
UK

First published in Vintage in 2022
First published in hardback by Chatto & Windus in 2021

penguin.co.uk/vintage

A CIP catalogue record for this book is
available from the British Library

ISBN 9781529113709

Printed and bound in Great Britain by Clays Ltd, Elcograf S.p.A.

The authorised representative in the EEA is Penguin Random House
Ireland, Morrison Chambers, 32 Nassau Street, Dublin D02 YH68

Penguin Random House is committed to a sustainable future
for our business, our readers and our planet. This book is made
from Forest Stewardship Council® certified paper.

MIX
Paper from
responsible sources
FSC
www.fsc.org
FSC® C018179

To Liz, the teacher of teachers,
and to Zoe, the one-woman Northern powerhouse,
and to all the teachers who do amazing work under
incredible pressure

Author's Note

In this book, I've recounted events from my teaching career based on my memories of that time. It goes without saying that the pupils and colleagues I had the privilege of working alongside are entitled to their privacy; for that reason names, other identifying features and locations have been changed throughout. On occasion it has also been necessary to merge certain individuals or situations to further protect identities. Any similarities are therefore purely coincidental.

Introduction

'You're brave,' is the commonest response when you tell people at parties that you're a teacher. 'Ooh, I couldn't do that,' comes a close second, and third, 'Is that what you always wanted to do?' – a thinly veiled attempt to ascertain what career you might have failed at previously to mean you ended up with this fate-worse-than-death job.

The public, by and large, speak to teachers in the same way they might address a despondent child who has just missed a shot at goal in an important football match. They search for words to put a positive spin on the situation, try to ignore the lingering sense of what might have been had the opportunity for success not been missed, and can't help but feel desperately sorry that things didn't work out for you.

It took me a while to get my head around that attitude, because I had always viewed teaching as the most desirable job in the world. While my classmates got Transformer figures or Barbies for their eighth birthdays, I got a full-size blackboard and a box of chalk. I spent hour after countless hour teaching imaginary figures the capital cities of the world or how to calculate the area of a rectangle. I created meticulous worksheets, called registers of names I had made up myself, and thought an ideal evening was marking imaginary work and giving encouraging feedback to non-existent pupils. Unsurprisingly, nobody ever accused me of being a cool kid.

It was rather an odd passion but perhaps it was in the blood; my dad taught music all his working life, and I loved watching him head out to school with his briefcase stuffed with exam papers, and return with stories of staffroom gossip and choirs that struggled to hold a note. I was lucky to have some larger-than-life primary school teachers, and their influence undoubtedly extended beyond the classroom walls. As far as I was concerned they were all-knowing figures, and I longed to emulate them.

But whatever the source of this enthusiasm, from as early as I can remember I was convinced that everyone must surely aspire to teach. I remember being genuinely perplexed as it slowly dawned on me that my classmates were not clamouring to forge a similar path.

Throughout a volley of careers interviews in secondary school and university, I remained stubbornly fixated. Many, many teachers told me that I should consider any other career path. 'The pay is terrible,' they would say, or, 'You should aim higher.' But nothing would deter me.

In fact, being taught by superb teachers at secondary school only cemented my ambition. I remember long summer afternoons in a balmy classroom with Mrs Webb teaching us *Macbeth*. Mrs Webb was statuesque and wore smart, flowing dresses. She was quietly spoken, and gave the air of gliding around the classroom as she mused on the folly of unchecked ambition or whether it was fair to blame the witches for Macbeth's demise.

Many an inexperienced, mischievous or lazy student thought that her slightly ephemeral nature meant she was a pushover. I remember one boy recounting an elaborate excuse about why he couldn't hand in his homework, which involved his sister's boyfriend's rabbit. With her voice barely above a whisper, Mrs Webb told him that she would expect the work to be on her desk before 9 a.m. tomorrow. Foolishly he opened his mouth to protest but got no words out before he was comprehensively shut down by a conversation-ending 'Tomorrow, please,' as she drifted out the door.

She was also generous with praise though, and I found myself trying harder and harder to impress her. Somehow even when she was criticising your work, you knew she was doing it because she wanted you to be better, and believed that you were. It was on one of those afternoons in Mrs Webb's company that I refined my career plan, and decided that I wanted to spend my life teaching English in secondary schools just like her.

When those phantom children of my home classroom became real ones, as I took up my first teaching post at the grand old age of twenty-two, nothing really threatened to remove teaching from the pedestal upon which I had placed it. Admittedly, marking work that contained actual writing took a little longer and was not always the recreational activity I would have chosen to fill my evenings, and real children tended to be slightly less compliant than invented ones, but this was still the pinnacle of everything I had hoped for from the working world. This was a job that was noble and chal-lenging, varied and fulfilling. And working with young people, whose minds were still being formed, who were unpredictable and curious and lively, and who always told you exactly what they thought, was the most ridiculous fun.

Of course, the honeymoon doesn't last for ever. There were times when teaching caused me great stress and frustration as well as joy. In the last decade the challenges facing schools, teachers and pupils have only increased. And yet, teaching is still a remarkable thing to do. All of our experiences are shaped by teachers, for better or worse, and their lessons and influence often echo through our lives.

What follows should therefore be seen as an ode to teaching, and the sheer pleasure of being in the classroom. Even amidst the difficulties, the pressures and the misfired lessons, there is nothing like it. This is a tribute to the extraordinary and largely unsung work done by teachers the length and breadth of the country every single day. I hope it lessens the supercilious smirk on the faces of those who think they're uproariously funny when they snort at parties, 'You know what they say – those who can't, teach.' But it's also a cry for help, because teaching is under attack like never before, and the idealism of the kid with the blackboard in the spare room was sorely tested over the years.

And So It Begins

It's September 2005, and a new cohort of pupils are anxiously making their way to their first day at school. Meanwhile the latest intake of trainee teachers are assembling for the first day of their new careers, feeling no less anxious than the children they are about to teach. The Faculty of Education where I will learn the ropes is a brand new, futuristic building on the outskirts of the city, and we're the first teachers to do our training there. It smells of paint and anticipation. Twenty or so of us are arriving for day 1 of a year-long course after which, with any luck, we'll be qualified to teach English in secondary schools.

The room is tense with expectation and I'm feeling that familiar 'first day' sense of shyness coupled with an urgent pressure to make friends. Like a gawky eleven-year-old boy who feels he should say something obscene to win mates, I attempt to ingratiate myself with my new-found colleagues by making an ill-advised, flippant comment about the North of England. Without a moment's hesitation a voice retorts, 'Oi, you'd better watch out, we're pretty hard in the North.'

The voice belongs to Zoe. She's a brilliant blonde ball of Northern energy. I like her instantly. As the weeks go on I learn that she's from Sheffield originally, but has landed down South to do her PGCE (Postgraduate Certificate in Education) after three years as an undergraduate at Durham. And she's every bit as fiery as her initial comment suggests.

The teacher training year is an odd mixture of quite easy university sessions which mostly involve arriving at ten and writing your feelings on Post-it notes, and school placements which can involve driving for hours to get to a godforsaken place at the crack of dawn to do a job you have no idea how to do, for no pay.

The particular challenge of a placement is that the kids know you're a student teacher and so the best you can hope for is that they take pity on you. Children, like animals, have a sixth sense for fear, and you have to pretend you're confident and authoritative, whilst demonstrably having no authority and severely lacking in confidence. We know that this won't be easy but I absolutely cannot wait. I have never been so sure that I am in the right place or on the right track.

A quick google tells me that the school I will be training at is located deep in the Cambridgeshire fens. I ask around and find out it's a school down on its luck, with low exam results and what is euphemistically referred to as 'challenging behaviour' lurking around every corner. Uneuphemistically it's called fights, bullying and general thuggery. The school serves a deprived area; many of the children there have never left the fens, or even been to their nearest city. As far as I'm concerned, that means there's all the more opportunity to make a difference. After only a couple of weeks of university-based preparation I am driving through the gates of the school for the first time and nothing can dim my excitement.

The plan is that I am to observe lessons for a week or so, then be gently eased in to teaching part-lessons under the supervision of an experienced teacher, getting feedback and improving as I go.

Much of my time in that first week is spent observing the lessons of a teacher called Tony. He is a very pleasant chap: tall, affable and with the slightly bumbling air of Hugh Grant playing an upper-class gent. But I quickly get the very distinct sense that the classroom might not be his natural habitat. He is also hard of hearing. I watch helplessly as children run rings around him, mouth words at him so that he thinks his hearing aid has broken, and pretty much rule the place.

I feel duty bound to make some notes in my brand new A4 binder which I have told myself will become a repository of wisdom on how to teach, but I don't really know what to write. 'Try not to lose all control'?

A week sitting at the back of Tony's classroom is, apparently, sufficient preparation: I am to be let loose on classes. And, it is explained to me, owing to some 'staffing problems' there will be no one supervising me. I will be alone with a group of thirty fourteen-year-olds, and I am to teach them *Richard III*. This is definitely against all the guidelines we were given at uni about how placements should work, but our cosy seminar room feels a world away from the front line, and the last thing I want to do is rock the boat. I have never read even a page of *Richard III*, so I start, with some urgency, to familiarise myself with it.

A Comedy of Errors

Despite how quickly this is all happening, I am beyond excited. For the first time there will be living, breathing children taking part in my lessons and they are blank canvases. My humble tools are the language and plots bequeathed to us by the Bard himself, and I will paint beautiful pictures in their minds and in their hearts. I spend hours of my weekend intricately planning the lessons. I run through them in my head over and over again. I stay up late into the night crafting handouts and activities and discussion topics. I think of the lessons I taught as a child to imaginary students – how well they always went, how everyone always paid attention and never answered back. The scenario which follows is a photographic negative of those lessons.

Ten minutes into the session my enthusiastic miming of Richard's hunchback is interrupted by Jade, a girl of fourteen who looks about twenty-five owing to a remarkably thick layer of make-up, saying, 'Sir, can I talk to you outside?'

'Of course,' I reply, grateful for even a moment in which I am not having to enact scenes that would leave Shakespeare aghast and complaining to Anne about how newbie English teachers persist in butchering his work.

'It's probably nothing,' Jade says, 'but I think Gavin fancies me.'

'I see,' I reply carefully. 'And is he being annoying?'

'Well, I'm just not really comfortable with how he's … like … *expressing* it.'

The next question is inevitable and yet nothing in me wants to ask it. 'What's he doing?'

It turns out that Gavin, who I had hitherto included among the good ones on account of the fact that he wasn't in open and total rebellion, has brought a pair of nail scissors with him to school. In his mind, it would be devastatingly seductive to trim himself down below, cut the hair up into a fine dust, and blow it into the face of an unsuspecting Jade, who was sitting opposite him. Jade had been busy at least pretending to listen to me explaining how much Richard's deformity must have made him feel like an outsider, when a pubic cloud had engulfed her.

I send Jade back into the classroom with entirely unsubstantiated assurances that I'll sort it out, and ask Gavin if I can have a word with him. As I remonstrate with young Gav that perhaps this is not the way to Jade's heart, I glance through the window in the classroom door. The class are not analysing the quotations I had given them to look at whilst I nip outside; they are instead setting upon two boys, beating them with rolled-up copies of the play.

'What are you doing?' I push open the door and shout with more desperation than authority in my voice.

'Just recreating the killing of the two young princes in the tower,' comes the reply, and sure enough they continue with their slaughter.

As I stand there, trying to explain why you shouldn't adorn your classmates with your pubic hair, whilst simultaneously attempting to save the two princes from their gang murder, I am struck by the realisation that this year is going to be harder than I had imagined.

Finding Your Persona

My first lesson was not, perhaps, the ideal introduction to teaching. I sit in the staffroom the next day, chatting to the Head of English, and carrying out a post-mortem. 'Remember', he says, 'if you can cope with teaching here, you'll cope with teaching anywhere.' It doesn't feel massively reassuring.

It was arrogant, of course, but I had envisaged myself taking to teaching like a duck to water, expecting that I would immediately become the version of myself I had spent so long imagining: relaxed and in control in the classroom, helping and inspiring children with the calm insistence displayed by Mrs Webb all those years before. I wanted to be Miss Honey, the perfectly quiet and kind teacher in Roald Dahl's *Matilda*, but in my first lesson I had felt like her frantic, ineffective evil twin.

I am trying to find my voice as a teacher, but some of the advice I receive is conflicting. Our tutor at uni is Christine, a brilliant, scatty, mildly chaotic former English teacher. We left the safety of her seminar room for our placements with her words ringing in our ears: 'Just be yourselves and you'll be fine.' But one stalwart of the staffroom has already taken me aside and told me in no uncertain terms not to smile in front of a class before Christmas.

I bump into Zoe in the university library one evening and ask her how she's finding it. 'Don't get me started,' she says. 'I can't deal with the *criers*. I kept three Year 7s who hadn't done a jot of homework behind the other day, and within fifteen seconds of opening my mouth to tell them off, all of them were in floods. Do you think I need to tone it down a bit?'

Clearly, finding our teacher personas is going to be a process of trial and error, with more error to come.

Yoga Therapy

Our time in our placement schools is broken up with days in college, on which Christine often models what a good lesson should look like, with us as the pupils. She has us acting out *Twelfth Night* as though it were an episode of *EastEnders*, and producing an episode of *Jeremy Kyle* featuring the characters of *Romeo and Juliet*.

In one of our sessions towards the end of November, Christine tells us that this is a difficult point in the course. Everyone is exhausted, Christmas is still a distant thought, and most of us are commuting significant distances to our placement schools. Staying up until the early hours poring over lesson plans has become the norm, as has lugging home folders full of work to be marked. One course-mate even buys a suitcase to transport it all, and has to deal with a constant stream of people asking her, 'Off anywhere nice?'

Christine tells us she's organised something that will help. She has booked a Swedish lady called Ulrika to lead a relaxation session. We traipse en masse, thirty trainee English teachers, down to the dance studio where Ulrika is waiting clad in luridly coloured Lycra, her curly hair pulled back with an eighties-style sweat band. She pops on a panpipes CD and, in her heavy accent, encourages us to 'lie dawwn on ze floooor and close your eyezzz'.

Before I'm really aware of what's happening I am, at Ulrika's instruction, on all fours, arching my back with my eyes closed and repeating over and over that 'I am accepting ze sunlight into my body'.

'You are now in a zstate of deeeeep relaxa-shon,' Ulrika tells us, although to be honest I can think of few scenarios which would correspond less with the feeling of relaxation than being screeched at by the female version of Mr Motivator whilst on hands and knees with my eyes closed. 'And naow,' Ulrika declares, 'you are on ze beach. Ze sun is beating down on your face. Per-aps ze school verk you av to do enters your mind for a zsecond. But you think, "Fack it."'

Maybe it's the sheer exhaustion. Maybe it's the entirely gratuitous swearing. Maybe it's just the ludicrousness of crawling around the floor with a group of grown adults. But someone next to me starts laughing. Not just a little titter, but a full-blown, uncontrollable, wheezing laugh. I open my eyes briefly and make eye contact with Zoe, whose facial expression is somewhere between discomfort, repulsion and outrage. And that's it. My knees go and I am flat on the floor, consumed with laughter. It spreads around the room and we end the session collapsed in a heap and gently convulsing. It is such a relief. And ironically, Christine and Ulrika have provided exactly what was needed, albeit not in the way that either of them intended.

We're All Learning

If I'm honest, by the time I'm a few weeks in, the training year is already proving tough. The hours are long and the workload for both school and college is huge, but when lessons go well, when kids wait behind to say that they enjoyed it, or have done some extra research that they proudly tell you about, that glow of satisfaction keeps you going. The Christmas holidays are within sight, but before they come I am to experience my first parents' evening. It's for Year 7, and I will shadow the class teacher as a succession of parents come and sit opposite us in the world's worst speed-dating session.

The teacher is Andrea, and she has been teaching for about five years. Andrea is brilliant. She is bright, welcoming and knows the kids – their strengths and weaknesses – inside out. I, on the other hand, have been in this school (any school!) for less than three months and still have times when I get lost on the way from the staffroom to the English department.

The parents on this particular evening fall into types. There are the earnest parents, making notes and bringing a list of pre-prepared questions. There are the harangued parents, who have clearly rushed from work and feel the need to sneak a look at their phone as if their emails might become unmanageable in the five minutes they are speaking to us. There are those who clearly try hard but find parenting really difficult, and ask for advice and help on how to raise their children. And there are those whose English isn't really up to a parent–teacher consultation.

One thing unites them. Over the course of the evening it becomes clear that they direct their eye contact, their questions, their observations to me and not to Andrea. They ask me – a twenty-two-year-old single man with no children who has worked in a school for about ten minutes – for advice. 'ASK HER!' I want to scream. 'I'M A TRAINEE! I HAVE LITERALLY NO IDEA WHAT I'M DOING.'

It goes to show that even in a line of work often seen as nurturing and traditionally female-oriented, sexism is so deeply ingrained that people still talk to the man as though he knows best. One dad, having looked at me the whole time, even when Andrea was speaking, turns to her before he leaves. 'What about you, love? Are you learning?'

Learning Lessons

Just as the memories of Gavin and his wooing techniques begin to fade, I learn another salutary early lesson about life at the chalkface: always, always take a breath before acting in anger.

I have picked up a Year 8 English class. My peers, who are completing their placements at other schools, are accompanied by the regular class teacher in their fledgling lessons. The teacher sits at the back, making notes and quietly quashing any behavioural issues that bubble up. The two then sit down and debrief over a civilised coffee.

But once again, owing to some undefined personnel issue, I am flying solo. There are vague apologies about this. There are compliments, the sole purpose of which is to pacify and appease: 'We're only doing this because you're definitely ready for it.' This is clearly just a lie, but I am too compliant and keen to please to challenge it.

The Year 8 class have been working on group presentations about poetic techniques. As they sidle to the front of the room in their clusters to deliver their insights, I am astonished to find that they aren't altogether terrible. But one girl in the last group worries me. Grace came to see me beforehand to say that she has a stammer and is really nervous about speaking out loud to others. We talked through her worries and I offered her all the reassurance I could muster, bearing in mind that I didn't really blame her for feeling anxious about standing in front of this lot.

As she takes her place by the board, about to give her talk, her eyes find me at the back of the room, and I nod and smile and try to look as enthusiastic and supportive as I can. Her breathing is erratic and she's clearly tense. Yet Grace explains what alliteration is. She gives examples. She talks about why a poet might use alliteration. And when she has finished, she beams.

It might seem like a small thing, but for Grace, this is a winning goal in a cup final, getting a Christmas number 1 and receiving a medal from the Queen all rolled into one. Her eyes go again to me, seeking reassurance, and I can't wait to tell her how brilliantly she has done. I share her sense of triumph and, although obviously the effort was all hers, I allow myself to believe that in a small way I've encouraged success.

A hand goes up. 'Josh, you want to say something?'

'I'd just like to say … G-g-g-g-good job, G-g-g-grace.' The classroom erupts with laughter, Grace's smile leaves her face and I feel a rage building inside me.

My words echo around the room: 'GET OUT, JOSH!'

In slow motion he gets to his feet and inches towards the door. We're talking a movement of a centimetre at a time. He could not move any slower without coming to a complete stop. He is doing it with the sole intention of winding me up, and I am playing into his hands. I am resentful that Josh has threatened Grace's already wafer-thin confidence and ruined a lesson which was actually going well, and I feel my hand rise to push him towards the door.

We have been told during our uni sessions that we should try to avoid touching a child for any reason because of the risk of it being misconstrued. So that means that if someone is crying you resist the natural urge to comfort them by putting your hand on their shoulder, and if a child tries to initiate a hug you politely decline. There are exceptions, of course; you can make contact to save a child from imminent danger to themselves or others. But physically ushering a child towards a door because they have annoyed you is definitely not covered by the exemptions. I am shocked and upset at my own lack of control.

Looking back, I can see that there were other factors at play too. I was an inexperienced trainee left to fend for myself, and being encouraged to run when I could barely crawl. There should have been somebody in the room, or at the very least on standby to offer support and advice with Josh.

I resolve that the next time Josh gets under my skin I will take five long, slow breaths before responding. Thank goodness some instinct kicked in and stopped me from pushing him that day. But it was close.

Pupil Pursuit

As the days and weeks roll by, and Christmas comes and goes, teaching slowly becomes more natural, and enjoyable. Where at the start of the placement I would be up all hours writing a script for each lesson, now I have faith that I'll be able to make it work using a basic plan. I no longer note down that a class discussion will take place between 11.03 and 11.08. I've learned to be a little more free and easy; to let a debate run on if it's going well or if someone has asked a really interesting question, or to cut it short if they're in a quiet mood, as classes are from time to time.

Early in the new year we're told that we'll be given the day off teaching to do something called a pupil pursuit. We'll each be allocated a child with a particular special educational need and we will follow them through their whole school day, moving with them through their lessons to try and get a sense of what their school life is like. My child is a Year 9 boy called Joe. He has dyslexia and finds it difficult to understand and respond to the verbal communication of others.

Our first lesson of the day is maths, and Joe has a learning support assistant allocated to him. She hovers nearby as he practises calculating probabilities, making sure he understands the language in some of the questions but giving him the independence to do the calculations himself. She helps him note down his homework and checks he knows where he's heading next.

It's music, and Joe has to do without an assistant here – he only has one for English and maths and even then only for some lessons. The class listen to some of Holst's *The Planets* and Joe joins in the discussion, but when the rest of them start a written task, I notice he really struggles to get started. From there we go through geography, PE, chemistry and German, him leading the way with me in tow. The special needs coordinator hadn't wanted to make him self-conscious so Joe isn't aware of what I am doing, but he must surely be wondering why on earth this weirdo keeps popping up wherever he goes.

By the end of the day I am so exhausted I can barely speak, and I've only been watching. It's a reminder of just how much kids are expected to do in a day; the sheer variety of topics covered, from tectonic plates to German verbs and the best technique to use when passing the ball in football. But beyond the content, Joe has been taught by six teachers, all with differing approaches and expectations, all fussing about the homework they are setting and the tests that are coming up and the progress students are making. He has targets to keep track of in all those subjects and others besides. It's a lot for anybody to deal with, but especially for a child with Joe's special needs. Teachers did their best to offer him individual support, but with twenty-nine others in the classroom, there is a limit to what they can do. It's invaluable for me, because I only see a child in my own lessons, and it's easy to forget that they have so much else going on in a day never mind a week.

If anyone ever tells you that kids these days have it easy in school, please know that you should probably not trust anything else they say. The child's-eye view is a revelation.

Taxi For One

I'm sitting in the staffroom writing an essay for my PGCE course when one of the teachers in the department pops her head around the door and asks me if I would mind supervising her class briefly. She tells me they're a wonderful class, they're just working silently and all I need to do is watch them for a few minutes while she attends to something urgent.

When I arrive at the classroom, I am not greeted by rows of silent pupils diligently getting on with their work. Instead almost all are talking, some loudly. Several are out of their seats and standing around in groups having a whale of a time. Not one is writing anything. I imagine their teacher coming back and seeing that I can't even control one of the best classes in the school.

'Ryan,' my internal monologue says, 'this is the time to act. Take decisive action to show you're in charge.'

In an out-of-body experience I hear myself say, 'What on earth is going on in here? I think we've had *quite* enough of that.' Silence falls instantly, and I can't believe that I've been so successful in bringing order so quickly. Maybe I am just a natural child whisperer?

But my smugness is interrupted by a student saying, 'But sir, our teacher is right there.'

With trepidation, I allow my eyes to move in the direction of his pointed finger. And there, sure enough, a senior teacher is standing, mouth slightly agape, brow furrowed. He is clearly wondering, not unreasonably, why a student teacher, himself barely out of puberty, has marched into his room and interrupted a lesson that was going perfectly well. I mutter something about needing to get back to the staffroom, and endure the walk of shame to the door. I am distantly aware of a voice shouting, 'Taxi for one!' as I leave.

I sit down in the classroom next door where, I need hardly tell you, the class are working in perfect silence, and reflect on the absolute necessity of never coming into contact with that teacher again.

Small People

I'm training to be a teacher of English in secondary schools, so will be teaching kids aged between eleven and eighteen. But it's a statutory requirement that you complete a week in a primary school as part of your training, working with children aged between four and eleven. So it is that I find myself on a crisp spring morning sitting on a very small seat, surrounded by very small people who are all staring at me – some with curiosity, more with thinly veiled displeasure.

I help with times tables and remember that nine sevens is still a struggle. I act as a special guest judge for show-and-tell reports. I join in with painting and, in a room of six-year-olds, my picture is in the lower half of the table for artistic merit. My overwhelming and lasting impression is just how high-pitched young children can be.

Some of the teachers shake their heads and say, 'I've no idea how you cope working with the big ones,' but the feeling is entirely mutual. For jobs that have the same title, they are remarkably different. For one thing, colleagues in primary schools teach all subjects, so they're expected to be as adept at science as they are at art. And if you think it's mostly easy kids' stuff, you mustn't have looked at any Key Stage 2 SATs papers lately. I couldn't tell you off the top of my head how many vertices a square-based pyramid has. And whereas we flit between classes and range across year groups, they have the same class more or less full-time for a year. Brilliant for getting to know the kids individually, but a nightmare if you have a difficult group.

As I walk home on my last day, wondering why every primary school teacher in the country has not been awarded the Victoria Cross for dealing with that much volume on a daily basis, I become aware of a presence to my left. I recognise the girl beside me as one of the Year 6 children I had been working with that day. Her name is Martha and she is ten, but a young ten. Her hair is in pigtails and I know from observing some of her classes that she is sparky, chatty and articulate. I ask her where she's heading.

'I'm walking home with you,' comes the response.

I laugh, presuming this is some kind of misfired joke. 'But where are you really going?'

'I want to come with you,' she says again, with no flicker of a smile.

My child protection training is ringing in my ears; this is a classic red flag of a child trying to push the boundaries which quite rightly exist between teachers and pupils. I tell her firmly that she won't be able to come home with me. As I inwardly congratulate myself on dealing with the situation professionally I hear her say, 'If you don't let me come home with you, I'll tell my teacher that you tried to touch me.'

It's the nonchalance with which she says it that is the most shocking thing. She has power in this new and terrifying situation, and she knows it. And the words hit home. 'I'm afraid that is a completely inappropriate thing to say, and I'm going to have to talk to the head teacher,' I somehow manage to reply. Martha shrugs and walks off. I stand alone in the street, my mind swirling with relief that the immediate situation has been defused, but also worry at what she's going to do now.

I phone the school immediately and the head suggests I walk back there to talk about it. Even I, a trainee, know how serious allegations of this nature are. They are often career-ending. And having something like this happen in your first term as a trainee must be some kind of record. Of course it is right that any child's accusation be taken seriously because the thought of them not being believed when there is genuine abuse taking place is too horrific to contemplate. But false accusations can be a terrifying experience for the adult involved.

The head teacher tells me this isn't the first time that Martha has made comments like this, and they have all been proved false. With every word she says I feel my shoulders start to relax. She tells me that she will speak to the girl and her parents and I never hear anything more of what happened. I return to secondary school, relieved that I won't have to see Martha again. Her threatened accusation never seems to materialise and I am quickly subsumed by the busyness of life in the classroom once again.

But I sometimes wonder about Martha. What could have happened in her life to make her say something like that? The head says that her family circumstances are complicated and she sometimes acts manipulatively, particularly with male staff. I imagine that men might have mistreated her in the past. She has sexual knowledge which is not age appropriate, and we have been told in our child protection training that can be a sign of abuse.

If I'm honest, my initial reaction to her threat was anger. How dare she risk my whole career by making up a lie? And all over something so trivial as whether I will walk with her. But as I think about it that evening and in the following days, in a more rational state of mind, I feel pity and empathy for Martha. She's only ten. Who knows what has happened to her in the past? It is not normal behaviour for a ten-year-old and likely some terrible thing has triggered it.

This is something I come back to again and again in teaching; the initial challenging behaviour tends to mask something deeper. I remember having various meltdowns when I was a kid over entirely inconsequential things like what we were having for dinner. It must have been irritating for my mother, but she listened patiently, let me get it all out of my system and then calmly asked what it was that was really bothering me. Invariably somebody would have said something at school that had upset me (it turns out this is not an infrequent occurrence for children who play with black-boards instead of footballs) and I would pour it out and feel a lot better afterwards.

I am not imbued with her levels of patience, sadly, but that lesson did stay with me. There are almost always reasons which explain why a kid is behaving poorly. It doesn't excuse their behaviour, or even mean that they shouldn't get in trouble for it, but I find it does help to temper your response.

Catcher

Back in the secondary school, and now towards the end of my placement, the evenings are getting longer and the sun is in the sky and things are looking up. Through necessity I've learned a great deal about how to manage a classroom.

Getting students into a routine is key, so they know that they have to come in, take a seat, get their book out and read quietly at the start of the lesson. It involves a bit of shouting initially and some huffing and puffing, but eventually they do it without me even having to speak. And I've learned to be clear that every student will start each new lesson with an entirely clean slate, no matter what has happened last time.

I've been given a Year 10 class and asked to teach them one of my favourite books, *The Catcher in the Rye* by J. D. Salinger. For the first time, the fates align, and it is an unadulterated joy. The kids adore the book. Some of them love Holden Caulfield, and identify with his insecurities and struggles. Others see him as aloof and hypocritical, and the debates are passionate and spirited. Kids come up to me in the corridors and the playground and the canteen to tell me their latest thoughts on what Salinger is saying through the text. I dig out old photos of me visiting some of the novel's settings in New York, and they are agog. I find myself looking forward to their lessons and, after a rocky few months, I am reassured that teaching truly is the best job going.

The End of the Beginning

Just like that, the training year is over and we are having drinks with Christine in the college garden. We're swapping stories of joy and woe, battles won and battles lost. One trainee took responsibility for the annual school play, a huge undertaking in any institution, and triumphantly pulled it off. Another managed to briefly leave a child in a motorway service station while driving a group to the theatre in the school minibus. I'm just happy to come out the other side relatively unscathed.

My view of teaching is slightly more realistic than it was when I first stepped into a classroom, nervously clutching my lesson plan and anticipating that the assembled teenagers would probably leave school that day determined to start their own Shakespeare company.

For all the challenges, I am feeling hopeful, excited and ready for what might come next. I've got a permanent job at a state school in a leafy market town. When I visited, it was clear it is a great school. The atmosphere is calm and purposeful, it has proper systems in place to deal with any misbehaviour that does occur, and it gets good results. I am looking forward to having my own classes rather than being thrown in to teach someone else's as a trainee. And even better, Zoe has got a job there too. I can't wait.

New Suits

Zoe and I decide to share lifts to our new school. It's a half-hour drive, and those journeys quickly become havens of joy at the start and end of every day. We share our tales about the hilarious things children have done and put the world, or at least the school, to rights.

We both buy new suits for our first day. Zoe is, as always, perfectly turned out, but my fashion sense is somewhat under-developed. We cut a slightly strange sight in my little Yaris. Think Marilyn Monroe and Jeremy Corbyn.

Still, we feel pretty good. We are strutting down the corridor past small huddles of children, trying to convey an air of calm authority and gravitas. We're talking about schemes of work and lesson plans and every so often saying, 'Good morning,' to students in the corridors. A more professional pair of teachers you could never hope to meet.

I am midway through a particularly pertinent comment about how we can make sure we cover all the relevant assessment objectives in A level lessons when it comes to my attention that Zoe is no longer beside me. I look behind and see her lying prostrate on the ground. Her new shoes may look smart but sadly they are no match for a highly polished floor. The tumble is clinical in its speed. We try to maintain our serious teacher faces as I bundle her up and we continue on our way, but both of us are suppressing giggles. When we turn a corner at the end of the corridor and the proper laughter comes it is uproarious and it continues more or less unabated every day for years to come.

Later that same day I am walking down the corridor behind two girls who look like they're probably in Year 9 or 10. I am not intentionally listening to their conversation, but they are not exactly speaking in hushed tones.

'Who have you got for English this year?' Girl A asks her friend.

'I've got that new guy, Mr Wilson – you know, the Irish one?' comes Girl B's reply.

'Oh yeah, I saw him from a distance. He looks fit.'

At this point in my eavesdropping I should do anything to get away from this exchange. Literally anything. Pretend I have forgotten something and walk the other way. Have a coughing fit. Begin a gymnastics routine right there in the corridor to stop their conversation.

Girl B raises her voice to a pitch that I didn't know humans were capable of, and screeches across the corridor, 'Are you actually joking? I think I might throw up even thinking about that.'

The First Lesson

I had imagined my first lesson as a proper teacher over and over in my head. I'd been dreaming about it since my eighth birthday. I pictured it being with a nice, easy Year 7 class who are as overawed as me. Instead I am starting with Year 13. At seventeen and eighteen these are the oldest students in the school and I am to teach them gothic literature.

My idea is to start by asking them to tell me their names and one thing they have done over the summer holiday. I begin by telling them all about visiting Rome (can you believe that the Colosseum was built in AD 80?) and then I turn to a student on my left and ask him what he got up to over the break. He looks me square in the eye and says, 'My name is Jack and I turned three straight men gay.' I make a mental note to stick to the syllabus in the next lesson.

But it's not only the fact that his inappropriate comment has derailed my much anticipated and entirely innocent icebreaker that leaves me feeling a little shaken. It's also how confident and at ease he is with his sexuality even at seventeen. I think back to my school experience where if anyone was remotely effeminate they were apparently fair game for every bully and thug in the vicinity. My discomfort is partly because Jack has reminded me that I will at some point have to deal with the open question of my own sexual orientation. But I decide to keep that buried for a while longer.

Unfair Cop

One fine autumn afternoon in that first September of my working life, in a sleepy Essex town, I nearly got arrested. I had been visiting family in Northern Ireland for the weekend, and had brought back a few of the local banknotes. Although perfectly legal tender in England, any Northern Irish person you speak to will have a litany of stories about the confused faces English shop assistants pull when you hand one of them over. So I decide to avoid all this hassle by nipping into town at lunchtime to get them changed.

I hand over the notes to the lady behind the desk in the post office, and she looks at me with barely concealed suspicion. 'We won't be able to do that,' she says with a curtness that should perhaps have been a warning sign. As I walk down the high street pondering where to try next, a police van draws up alongside me. Four policemen jump out and surround me. It's funny how your mind works when you're suddenly accosted like that. I drove through an amber-but-could-maybe-be-red light about two weeks ago and now I assume that my rakish ways have finally caught up with me.

Just as I am preparing to confess to my driving sin and graciously accept my penalty points with profuse apologies, one of the officers tells me, in the tone of voice you normally reserve for telling someone in a shop that there is a queue, actually, that they are investigating a serious case of fraud and need to speak to me. He asks me whether I have anything on my person that he should know about. I do a mental check of what I've got in my pockets. Several red pens, my house keys, and some flyers for the school play ... I think there can't be anything too incriminating there. And then it dawns on me.

'I do have about two hundred pounds of Northern Irish banknotes,' I state somewhat sheepishly.

'Not looking good, is it, sir?' is his stark response.

A full body search ensues in the middle of the high street. If they are hoping for a high-octane, *CSI*-style bust, they are going to be disappointed. The only dramatic moment involves one officer feeling something in the pocket of my oversized blazer and asking, 'What is this, sir?' He seems disappointed to discover that it isn't a revolver or a pistol, but a board marker.

As they leave, having found nothing more incriminating than a bit of extra cash, the lead policeman says something about how the lady in the post office had mistaken me for an Irish guy who was known to be laundering money. One of them tells me he has been trying to get tickets for the school play which his daughter is in but that it is sold out, and I promise him I will see what I can do. And as they get back in their van I look to my right and see that a group of sixth form students who I teach have witnessed the whole thing. The humiliation is complete.

The Professional Mentor

New teachers like Zoe and me have weekly meetings throughout our first year. They're a chance to share battle stories and get peer advice from others who are facing similar challenges. There are about twelve of us from different subject areas at these meetings, and each week has a different focus, anything from pastoral care to literacy.

Presiding over these meetings is Liz. She's an experienced teacher of French and German. She's also one of the best people you could ever meet. Her official title is professional mentor, but she is more like a mother. Or a god. Every week she is waiting with reassuring, practical words of advice which make everything seem doable. She is as warm as anyone I've ever met, but she has a core of steel and can cut through nonsense and jargon like nobody else. And man, does she love teaching.

Later that term the school holds a careers fair for sixth form students, and I happen to be with Liz listening to a talk about getting into teaching. The speaker is jaded and cynical, and suggests to the group they'd be better off trying something else. Liz marches to the front and takes over, giving an off-the-cuff speech which amounts to a love letter to the teaching profession. When she finishes the students clap, and the original speaker is left wondering what force of nature she has just encountered.

At one of our early meetings, it quickly becomes clear that Liz has got wind of my brush with the law. She regales the others with the story, telling it with verve and humour, but somehow without making me the butt of the joke. So much of teaching is about being able to communicate effectively, and it is clear right from the start that she's a master.

Norwich

Zoe has been staying at a friend's house while she's having some work done on her flat, and I pick her up there one morning. We are busying ourselves doing impressions of one of the senior leaders when it occurs to me that I have assumed that Zoe knows the way to our workplace in Essex from her friend's house in Cambridge, while she has assumed that I do. The upshot is that we end up somewhere near Norwich. I have no doubt that Norwich is a beautiful place, but it has the significant disadvantage of being really quite far from where we work.

Zoe makes a rather undignified call to our boss who is good enough to supervise our first classes of the day until we make it in a little late. Sadly he isn't good enough to keep the reason for our lateness secret. My class have drawn a map on the board by the time I get there and they cheer and whoop as I half-heartedly try to convince them that my car just wouldn't start.

In Praise of Eccentricity

I am assigned a personal mentor who I can look up to, and emulate. Where Liz is the professional mentor, and leads the group sessions for new teachers, this is meant to be someone from whom I can learn more about the pastoral side of the job. His name is Robert Clements and he teaches design and technology. 'Sergeant Clements' the kids call him, and he does have the air of a military man about him. His teaching style is … unique. During my first session observing him, he's meeting some of the GCSE students from his form group to go through their recent report cards.

'YOU KNOW WHAT REPORTS ARE?' he bellows at one timid lad. 'REPORTS ARE A THERMOMETER. THEY ALLOW US TO TAKE THE TEMPERATURE OF HOW YOU'RE DOING. SO LET'S SUCK THE THERMOMETER TOGETHER.' The boy shows remarkable forbearance as a high-volume critique of his report card takes place only inches from his face. 'LOOK AT YOUR CHEMISTRY RESULT. YOU KNOW WHO'S BEEN VISITING YOU, DON'T YOU?' A long pause. 'YOU'VE BEEN VISITED BY CAPTAIN COCK-UP!'

Watching Robert teach is nothing short of extraordinary. He marches around the workshop castigating and praising in equal measure.

'YOU'RE A DEMON WITH THAT SAW, JONES. BETTER NOT GIVE YOU A LOW MARK OR YOU MIGHT SLICE ME IN TWO.'

'WATKINS, WHAT IS THAT? CALL THAT A JEWELLERY BOX? I WOULDN'T PUT MY ROTTEN APPLE CORE IN IT.'

On one occasion he asks me to cover his form time for him: basically turn up, read out the announcements from the daily bulletin, call the register and send the students on their way. I walk through the door of his workshop to find he has written on the board, 'MR WILSON WILL TAKE FORM TIME TODAY AND HE' – and this was written in even bigger letters – 'EXPECTS SILENCE.'

That may all sound a little exhausting, but here's the thing: he really cares about the students in his form. And his DT classes love his lessons. For all his blustering and shouting he is a brilliant teacher. His sense of humour means he can turn even the most cack-handed of students into carpenters. He is unconventional, but there's no doubt he is one of life's natural teachers.

Clements retired after I'd been at the school for a couple of years, and there was a real sense that we had lost one of the last of the old guard. In my experience, the number of eccentric teachers has come down drastically. Schools have changed. Whereas at one time teachers were trusted to get on with their job, there are now appraisals, observations, learning walks and management drop-ins. Teachers are expected to create lesson plans for every lesson, drawing on student data and dividing the learning into phases and stretching the most able while supporting those who struggle most. Large, sponsored academy chains have taken many schools further down the road of privatisation, and made them more slick, more corporate.

There are reasons for all these things. League tables, funding cuts, forensic inspections and exam pressures mean that schools have had few options but to change. But those changes come at a cost. I have seen brilliant colleagues pushed, blinking and disorientated, into an unfamiliar and uncomfortable new world of hyper-accountability. Experienced teachers who have spent years honing their craft are ushered into empty classrooms or offices to be told that, regretfully, they are being put on a capability plan because they haven't made enough use of data or their lesson plans aren't sufficiently detailed.

The problem is that eccentric teachers are often brilliant. I'm not saying there aren't duds; there are in any profession. But when I think of my own school days, it's the characters I remember most vividly. I can't call those times to mind without thinking immediately of Mrs Weir, a larger-than-life maths teacher, whose world was so filled with theorems and formulae that she had never heard of Madonna, but who could make double maths pass in a flash. Or Miss White, the religious education teacher who told the girls not to shine their shoes too much in case they reflect their knickers and lead the boys into temptation, and Mrs Reid, our Year 5 teacher, who would throw our possessions out of the window if we misbehaved.

These teachers might not be able to provide a seating plan annotated with the different levels that their students are working at. But they are the inspirers, the ones who make learning effective as well as memorable and fun, and any system which is too inflexible to accommodate them deprives itself of some of the best.

Feeling Deflated

Zoe and I look at one of the tyres on my car, and wonder out loud whether it might be flat. We pull into a garage on our way to school to investigate further. It would be difficult to imagine two people less suited to fixing a flat tyre. Zoe is in heels and panicking about her hair being ruined by the moderate breeze. I can only just about identify which bit of the car the tyre is. We stare at the wheel for quite a while. We both frown at it. Zoe half-heartedly jabs an immaculately shoed toe at it. And we are none the wiser.

By this stage, we have perfected walking around school as if we are actual authority figures, and even manage to stay upright while doing it. But this is a reminder that outside the school gates it doesn't take long for the mask to slip.

We drive on and hope for the best.

Shakespeare

I have a lovely, sparky, alert Year 8 class and am charged with teaching them *Much Ado About Nothing*.

'This term we're going to be reading a play by Shakespeare,' I tell them jauntily. 'I wonder whether anyone in the room knows of any other plays that were written by William Shakespeare?' A sole hand goes up. 'Go ahead, Ben.'

'I'm not one hundred per cent sure. But I'd say I'm ninety-nine per cent sure there's one called *James and the Giant Peach*.'

We have some way to go.

Too Much Data

Zoe and I are slowly drowning under an ever growing pile of student data. If you've never been a teacher, or haven't spent a lot of time in schools in recent years, you might be unaware of the tyranny of data that is oppressing the profession. In September, along with your new planner and, if you're lucky and the budget will stretch, a board pen, you receive a wodge of statistics about every student you will be teaching. All the scores from public tests they've done over the years, all the results of internal tests which are designed to show aptitude, the level they were working at when they arrived at the school, the level they're supposed to be working at by the time they leave ...

You're expected to deploy this arsenal of numbers in every lesson you teach. So your lesson plan should say things like 'When asking questions about why Atticus agreed to defend Tom Robinson in *To Kill a Mockingbird*, consider asking Alexis because her verbal CAT score of 120 suggests she should be stretched more.' That's insanely time-consuming, but you could potentially argue the benefits of using stats strategically like that.

The killer is that you're expected to *add* to this avalanche of data. As often as every six weeks you have to sit down and enter the level at which little Jonny is performing, often using decimal points although quite what a national curriculum level 4.4 looks like, or how it differs from a 4.3, isn't clear to anybody as far as I can tell. The golden rule is that the numbers have to be getting better otherwise the spreadsheet turns red and you're expected to do something about it.

Now the first point to make is that the idea that children make steady progress every six weeks is a nonsense. Is a child who produced a mediocre essay on *Noughts & Crosses* in March likely to have radically changed ability by April? Pretty unlikely. Even the best teachers can't force all children to develop to a schedule like that. But you have to play along with the charade.

And let's say their performance is quite different from one half-term to another. Well, you might have been doing essay-writing skills one half-term and studying and writing poetry the next – so the change of level isn't necessarily a sign of progress, it's just that it's a very different skill being tested.

The result of the imperative for constantly improving data is almost meaningless data. And yet teachers spend hours of their time entering it into the data management system for each of their classes. Management teams then spend hours poring over it, looking for worries or anomalies, and heads of department are all too often expected to lay on extra sessions to address concerns.

A lot of this is driven by worries about critical reports from Ofsted (the Office for Standards in Education, Children's Services and Skills), the pantomime baddie of the educational world. The consequences of such a report can be enormous. Head teachers can come under pressure to resign. Almost inevitably, morale among staff and children plummets. Recruiting great teachers becomes more difficult. Ofsted can return more frequently to see whether things are improving, meaning everyone is constantly looking over their shoulders, wondering whether today will be the day they show up. In the worst-case scenario, it can be the start of a downward spiral for schools.

In idle moments I let my mind wander to what schools would be like if teachers were freed from all data obsession. Just think of all the extra time that teachers could spend on planning exciting, dynamic lessons. Leadership teams could work on ideas which would help support their teachers. Heads of department could get on with actually being good managers. It goes without saying that tracking students' progress is important. But as the old adage has it, you don't fatten a pig by weighing it more often.

Parents' Evening

Whenever the nonsense of the education system seems too much, it's time to pause and remember the joy of actually being in the classroom. I have a wonderful Year 12 class. They're attentive but questioning, enthusiastic but committed, and it's a pleasure to be in their company. Sometimes I can turn up to a lesson with a broad question linked to what we're studying, throw it out there, and allow them to spend the next fifteen or twenty minutes debating it, challenging one another, putting forward their own ideas, revising those ideas in the light of others' views and coming to a joint conclusion.

Their interest is energising, and their receptiveness means that every lesson feels productive and worthwhile. Any time someone at a party makes a negative comment about teaching, I think of this group of young people and I know that there's nowhere I'd rather be.

The only problem is with a boy called David. If ever there's even the slightest possibility of innuendo in anything we're reading he dissolves into laughter. It doesn't help that we're studying *Death of a Salesman* by Arthur Miller, with its tragic hero Willy Loman. After a few times saying naively, 'Right, I need a Willy,' when trying to find volunteers to read that part, I learn my lesson.

It's my first parents' evening flying solo, and I can't wait to tell the people responsible for bringing up these young adults that they've done a brilliant job. David is sitting opposite me, flanked by his mum and dad. If you've had the pleasure of attending one recently, you'll probably know that these days it's the norm for the students to attend parents' evenings too.

'David is just a delight to teach,' I hear myself innocently say. 'He always contributes to the discussions we have in class and that's so positive for everyone. The beauty of it is that he stimulates himself but he also stimulates every other person in that room.'

David raises an eyebrow and I struggle to suppress my laughter enough to continue speaking.

Not Your Friend

I have a child called Patrick in my Year 9 class. He invariably sits with his head on his desk, yawns every few minutes, and has rarely if ever produced anything resembling home-work. I'm worried that he's not learning and he's not going to be ready for the GCSE course next year. I bite the bullet and call home. Here's how the conversation goes:

'Hello there. My name is Ryan Wilson and I'm calling from Patrick's school. I'm his English teacher. It's just that I've noticed that Patrick seems to be tired a lot of the time. He's quite lethargic, he seems to struggle to do his home-work and sometimes it feels like he's even falling asleep in class. I wanted to see if we could have a chat about that?'

'Oh, tell me about it. It does our heads in too. I'll tell you what the problem is, Mr Wilson. He sits up most of the night and plays his Xbox. We sometimes go in there and find him playing it at three or four in the morning.'

'Oh, really? Well, that's pretty clearly at the root of the problem then.'

'Yes, it is. And I've had a chat with him about it. The thing is we have a brilliant relationship. We're like best friends. We can talk about anything.'

'Well, it's good he feels he can talk to you. What did he say?'

'He just explained how much he loves his video games. They really bring him so much pleasure. He's very good at them, you know.'

'I'm sure. It's just that it's really having a negative impact on his schoolwork. This morning he could barely lift his head off the desk.'

'Bless him. He does stay up too late playing them.'

'Do you think maybe we could try taking the Xbox off him for a period, and seeing how that affects things?'

'Ooooh, I don't think so. He wouldn't like that at all.'

And so the conversation descends into a farcical spiral, where we agree that a problem exists, and agree on its cause, but the parent won't commit to a possible solution because the child might not like it.

This desire a minority of parents have to be best friends with their offspring is one that I confess to finding a little odd. Your best friend, surely, is Dave who you go to the pub with on Fridays, or Lisa who you were at college with and still see every week at aerobics? The idea that you could be best friends with your twelve-year-old son has to be misguided. You wouldn't tell Dave that he was having no more beer unless he apologised for his behaviour, or Lisa that she wouldn't be seeing her sweat band again until she saw the error of her ways, but you sure as hell should tell Patrick that he's not having his Xbox back until he learns to control his use of it.

It's a trend I notice from time to time in teachers too, the desire to be mates with their students. But in my experience children hate it when you try to be pally. In fact they'd much rather have a very strict teacher than a friend. They like boundaries, they like knowing where they stand and yes, they even secretly like being told they can't do something when they know deep down it's in their own interest not to do it.

One teacher who definitely doesn't try to be matey with the kids is Zoe. Her Yorkshire accent makes her dismissals all the more potent. 'I can assure you he does not need a TV in his room. If you ask me you should get rid of it, Mrs Quinn, and do yourselves and him a favour.' The more bluntly she speaks, the more students and parents alike adore her.

Changing Rooms

The head of PE sends an email to the entire school's staff. He thought that we might like to know that Jake in Year 9 spent the first five minutes of his lesson with his PE top over his head struggling to find the armholes. Only after his teacher's intervention was it discovered that poor old Jake had inadvertently packed a pillowcase instead of a T-shirt in his PE bag that day.

The Gothic

Meanwhile I am continuing to struggle with my Year 13s, who are not the easiest bunch to teach. Ever since Jack announced his summer conquests in that first class, they have gone out of their way to make life difficult, turning up halfway through lessons with an unapologetic shrug, arguing with each other and with me, and taking any chance they get to undermine me. It's particularly hard because I am only a few years older than them, and I'm sure that's a contributing factor. I do my best to hide any frustration and stay positive in how I speak to them, but it isn't always easy.

There is a weird alchemy involved in classroom dynamics. None of these students are unpleasant or obstructive on their own. You wouldn't necessarily look at the names on the register and think, 'That's a nightmare group.' But whereas the Year 12 class spark off each other, take ideas and run with them and encourage each other to be better, this group does the opposite. It's also a bit embarrassing because you might expect to struggle to control a big Year 9 class, but fifteen Year 13s are supposed to be a breeze.

We are learning about gothic literature and I have them writing essays most weeks on some aspect or other of the genre's characteristics. One fateful week, instead of asking them to produce an analysis of *Frankenstein* or *Dracula*, I decide to let them instead write their own gothic short story. The idea is that they can showcase everything they have learned about the genre whilst having a more creative outlet than just deconstructing someone else's book.

As I mark their work that evening I am pleasantly surprised to see they have clearly absorbed some of the classic tropes of gothic writing. They are including vulnerable lone females, interweaving supernatural elements with the plot and giving their writing as much realism as possible in order to evoke fear or trepidation in the reader. Then I come to Sarah's story.

Sarah has taken against me from the start. Her reason for this is unclear but her commitment is impressive. She is argumentative and comes up with excuse after excuse for not producing any work. Exasperated, I tried calling home to see if her parents could help chivvy her along a little. They were supportive and said they would do what they could to help. But Sarah did not like that one little bit.

Her gothic story is about a girl called Zara who didn't do much work in her English lessons. Zara was able to get away with it, though, because even though her English teacher, Mr Williams, was frustrated with her and even tried calling home, ultimately he needed to admit to himself that he was 'addicted to Zara's perky thirty-two double Ds'. It didn't incorporate many of the traditional elements of the genre but if the point of a gothic story is to make the reader's blood run cold, I suppose Sarah succeeded.

I speak to the head of sixth form about Sarah's short story the next day and in the end they take her out of my class. It's sad really. Teaching is all about building positive and professional working relationships. Even when the students are difficult, it's your job to be the 'parent', to rise above it, and to find a way to make it work. With Sarah, for some reason, I wasn't able to do that, and the Zara essay was the final straw. For all her exterior confidence, bluster and hard appearance, I suspected she was a troubled girl. Her aggression seemed out of all proportion. I just regret not being able to find a way to get past her outward defences and bring her on side.

Shortly after this incident, Sarah's time at the school comes to an abrupt end due to some complications at home. I can't help but feel that I have failed her.

Suburban Thuglife

Sean, a boy in my Year 10 GCSE group, is what passes in leafy suburbia for a thug. Or at least he thinks he is. He's part of the closest thing the school has to a gang. They swagger round, shirts perpetually untucked, causing moderate amounts of trouble. We're not talking about international drug cartels or organised crime. Think more like the occasional cheeky fag in the bushes at the end of the playing field and setting up an illicit business selling sweets of dubious origin.

In my lessons Sean generally sits with his head slumped on the desk, and no amount of cheery encouragement will rouse him. In fairness, though, at least that is not disruptive. When he wants to he can derail a carefully crafted lesson in five seconds flat. On one occasion it happened when Juliet first appeared on screen in Baz Luhrmann's *Romeo and Juliet*. All it took was a well-timed 'I would' and all hell broke loose.

Sean is a pain. He's uncooperative and I sense the other kids feel impeded when he's in the room. But he's not unkind and it's impossible to really dislike him. One day he hangs back after a lesson to talk to me. The idea that he might be about to ask for some extra reading suggestions runs briefly through my head. Instead he leans in conspiratorially and asks, 'Sir, are you interested in DVDs? I'll do you a copy of *Knocked Up* for two fifty.' I politely decline.

The best evidence that Sean is not really the gangster he fashions himself as comes just before Christmas. As it's the last lesson before the holidays we're playing a class game of *Family Fortunes*, and it's girls against boys. The scores are level pegging and it all comes down to the final question. It's Sean who's up next. 'We asked a hundred people ... what is the first thing that touched your lips this morning?' My mind races at what inappropriate answers he could come up with, but actually the top answer is cigarette, so I reckon he may just get it right. He's thinking ... he's a little panicked ... all eyes are on him. The hopes and dreams of his teammates rest on his shoulders, and you can tell he feels the pressure. Finally he blurts out his answer. 'Advent calendar chocolate?' I suspect that if Sean actually met some proper thugs he wouldn't last very long.

Projection Error

I think that maybe showing Year 9 some of the brilliant *Richard III* film adaptation starring Sir Ian McKellen might help to bring the play to life. The school has just installed projectors in every classroom so I can show it on the big screen. I forget that there is a (mercifully not overly graphic) oral sex scene at one point. In desperation I throw myself between the projector and the screen to block their view. All that happens is the scene is projected onto my face. The students think this is the funniest thing that has ever happened. On the way home, through unabating laughter, Zoe tells me I am a pillock.

Getting Iso

My school, like many comprehensives, operates an isolation room. The idea is that kids who have been particularly poorly behaved can be sent there for anything from half a day up to two or three days. Sean, for example, is no stranger to it. 'See ya later, mate, I got iso,' is the standard farewell I hear him bid as he sidles off there.

In recent times the use of isolation rooms has become somewhat controversial. Mothers in local newspapers glare out from photographs, their arms around their equally rage-filled children. They complain that what's been done to their little cherubs violates their human rights.

The picture these mothers, and certain elements of the press, conjure up is reminiscent of the chokey in Roald Dahl's *Matilda*: a ten-inch-square cupboard with broken glass protruding from the walls and nails on the door, where recalcitrant children languish until they have learned their lesson. Before I visit our school's isolation room, I think of it as a Victorian-style workhouse serving up gruel. I find that the reality is rather different.

It's a comfortable and well-equipped classroom, presided over by senior staff. Four or five children sit at individual desks with small screens between them to stop them leaning over and chatting to each other, and they take lunch and break at different times of day from the rest of the school so that they aren't subsumed into the general melee. They're all getting on with work that has been set for them by their teachers. Before they are allowed back into lessons they'll have a reintegration meeting with whichever member of staff or pupil they had their run-in with. It's all very civilised, and it's difficult to reconcile the scene in front of me with the vitriol that some campaigners feel for isolation policies.

The kids here are not being neglected; on the contrary they've got a much better adult:child ratio than they would have in any classroom. They have breaks, they get time to reflect on their behaviour and they don't even fall behind with their schoolwork. And isolation is an alternative to formal exclusion, so they also won't have that on their record. Just as crucially, the other children in their class and, lest we forget, the teacher, will have some respite from that child, and a lesson or two which can proceed without disruption.

Only heads of year and senior leaders have the power to sentence students to isolation, so that mitigates the risk of individual teachers being a little over-zealous with their sanctions. Swearing at teachers is automatic iso. Fighting is almost always iso. A repeated pattern of smaller things like lateness or failure to attend detentions can also end up in iso. I have referred pupils for all those things. It teaches them that their actions have consequences.

So I'm not really sure that the Court of Human Rights will have too much interest in the case of little James who has to sit in a nice room doing work on his own for half a day because he decked someone. Despite what his angry mother would have us think, it is not one of the great injustices of our time.

Walkin' Wavy

My GCSE class are studying *A View from the Bridge* by Arthur Miller. It's a total joy to teach, and has the advantage of not having any Willys. Instead there is Eddie, the rough-and-ready New York longshoreman who the kids instantly take to, along with his long-suffering wife Beatrice. We imagine what they might be like if they lived in modern-day Essex. The kids take it in turns to pretend they are the characters and take questions from the floor, and we create our own episodes of *EastEnders* based on the plot, just as Christine taught me.

But although the class is engaged and interested and responsive to the whole play, the bit which sets the room alight is Eddie's relationship with Catherine, his niece by marriage. He is extremely protective of her; he scrutinises what she is wearing, he tells her off for 'walkin' wavy' down the street and he seems to be annoyed when she talks to other men. I cautiously moot the idea with the class that maybe Eddie's interest in Catherine might be more than avuncular. The room erupts. They are stamping their feet, banging their desks and cheering. As I struggle to bring them back to order, I console myself that at least it's the ideas in the play that are animating them.

A few days later a lady comes up to me in the canteen and introduces herself to me as Caroline. She says she teaches maths in the school. I am returning the introductions when she interrupts to say that she knows all about me because her son Matt is in my GCSE group. As we walk back towards the main school together, she says some lovely things. She says Matt has never really enjoyed English before but now he comes home and talks about his lessons. He is more motivated and talks about how he is planning to go all out to get an A. She says that English is now one of his favourite lessons, and that she can't thank me enough.

I am really touched by what she says, but conscious that there are all sorts of factors at play: he has quite a few friends who have ended up in the same class as him which obviously means he enjoys the lessons more, and the class is reasonably small so he can get a lot of attention. Plus I am not very good at dealing with praise. So rather than just saying how glad I am to hear it, I try to bat the compliment away.

'Well, it's very kind of you to say so, but I think it's just that they're quite into the play we're studying at the moment,' I tell Caroline. The next bit comes out of my mouth without me thinking about what I'm saying even for a moment. 'There's a bit of incest in it, and I think that's what he likes.'

Did I just tell the mother of a boy I teach that he enjoys a bit of incest? Yes, I think that's what happened. And now we're at the end of the corridor and going our separate ways, so there isn't even time to elaborate or explain. Caroline's forehead is a little contorted, as if she is wondering whether she could have heard correctly. My mouth is opening and closing but emitting no sound as I come to terms with the full horror of what I have just said. Caroline quietly responds, 'Well anyway, nice to meet you.'

And with that she is gone and I am alone again with my shame.

French Verbs

Liz has set our group of newbie teachers a challenge: find another teacher outside your own subject area who you admire or look up to, and ask them if you can come and watch their lesson. Too often we get stuck in our own class-rooms, she says, and we get busy, and therefore we don't reflect or innovate or improve. She's absolutely right, of course. Everyone is working all hours, and it feels as though getting on with marking or planning would be the best use of any free time we do get in the school day, but unless we carve out some space to improve our practice we won't be reaching our full potential as teachers.

As I consider the teachers I could approach, I keep coming back to one idea: the only person I really want to see teach is Liz. I catch her in the corridor and ask whether I might be able to come and observe one of her classes some day. She beams and says she's extremely flattered and we put a date in the diary.

It is her Year 8 French group I'm watching. To see her in action is like watching Picasso dancing his paintbrush against a canvas, or Mozart arranging his notes. They say teaching is an art, and Liz is an artist par excellence, if you'll pardon my French. She greets all thirty children by name with a jolly '*Bonjour*' as they come in. She asks one if they are feeling better. She congratulates a second on their success in the football team. She takes another to task over their untucked shirt but cheerily and in such a way that they smile as they comply.

I find navigating the line between being friendly and being strict difficult. I started off trying to be strict, but found it's not really my style. And I've tried being smiley and pleasant only to find that the kids take advantage and then I am left having to shout and threaten just to try and pull things back. But Liz walks that particular tightrope with ease, and doesn't even break a sweat doing it. She is no pushover and she isn't afraid to tell them off when they need it. But she is so warm, so interested in them and their lives, so effortlessly in command, that they gladly take it from her.

She has planned an exercise to teach the class about conjugating verbs. Under a lesser teacher this would be utter drudgery. With Liz, the class are hanging on her every word. She projects sentences onto the board with gaps for the students to choose the correct part of the verb, but the sentences refer to the kids in the class. They make reference to Tim forgetting his homework again, or Amelia practising her ballet, or the time that Elliott got that unfortunate haircut. They praise or they describe or they gently tease individuals, and it is genius. They can't wait to see what will come up on the screen next, they glow when it's their moment in the sun, and they don't even realise they are learning about French verbs. At one point, she asks them, 'Remember, what's the thing to say to sound French?' All around me, there is a chorus of '*Alors, euhhhh,*' as they give their best elongated French noises.

It's only when our group of newly qualified teachers next meets that I learn that nearly all of us chose to go and observe Liz. I was about the tenth person to approach her and ask whether I could come along and watch her, but she never even mentioned that. She just graciously agreed and set about arranging a time.

The kids might have learned about French, but I'm reflecting on how to make every child feel like they're really part of a lesson, that they are valued regardless of their ability, and how to effortlessly combine authority with friendliness.

A Coursework Miracle

Sean – the resident wannabe hard man of my GCSE group – will have to produce five pieces of coursework at home for his English GCSE. His creative writing piece is, naturally, late and I keep him behind in order to use all my powers of persuasion, encouragement, bribery and emotional manipulation to get him to do it.

It had been a great unit to teach. We read together a chapter of Bill Bryson, where he describes arriving in England for the first time. We discussed how he made his descriptions so vivid, how he used humour to engage the reader and how he varied his sentence structures to keep his writing interesting. And then they set about doing their own piece of travel writing. I made it clear it didn't have to be a fancy holiday; they could just as easily describe going to the shops if they picked up on all the little details and made me feel like I was there experiencing it with them.

Lo and behold Sean appears at the staffroom door the next morning and asks to see me. 'I've got that thing you wanted,' he grunts. I briefly consider explaining to him that it's not so much that I want it as that he needs it, but think better of that. I am internally congratulating myself that my supplications have borne fruit against the odds, while Sean rummages through what appears to be his PE kit.

'It's in here somewhere,' he mutters. From deep within his trainer, Sean pulls a single crumpled sheet of paper with

67

two and a half lines of writing on it. I hold it gingerly by the corner while trying to conceal my disappointment. It reads, 'I went to Harlow. I drove their with my mum. We saw my cousin and played Xbox. She won and I got annoyed.'

Must Do Better ...

Writing reports is part of the rhythm of school life. And they are done in volume. Every child gets a full report once a year, and progress checks twice a year. Progress checks contain data like estimated grades and effort levels, while reports have formal written comments. Let's just focus on the reports for a minute. If you have seven classes averaging twenty-eight pupils in each, you're looking at nearly two hundred full reports to write every academic year. In those subjects with less contact time for younger students, like art and drama, you could easily have fourteen classes, so you're at nearly four hundred reports a year before you even consider the progress checks.

They try to spread them out across the year so that you aren't writing them for your Year 7s at the same time as your Year 12s. But the result is a Forth Bridge scenario where you are in a permanent state of report writing, and by the time you've done the last ones, you're going back to the start again.

As I sit down to write my first set of reports, the school's instructions come as a bit of a surprise. There is space on the report form for you to enter a grade, and marks for effort, but it's the comment section that throws me. You have to write a few sentences about 'positive personal achievement' – what the student has done well. Fair enough. The only other box is for a target: a positively phrased suggestion of what the student should do to improve.

I fully understand the principle behind the positivity, and I'm on board with it in theory. It's great to build self-esteem, and if students feel that they're doing well and making progress, it often becomes a self-fulfilling prophecy. I think that's a useful guide, and in the majority of cases it's the right thing to do. But there are times when it would be helpful to signal to parents that there is a problem. Increasingly I'm learning that schools do not think guiding principles are enough; they must be reframed as hard rules. So you are no longer allowed to say anything that might be perceived as negative.

When I was at school I remember the teachers saying, 'Unless you buck your ideas up, you'll be getting a bad report,' and that felt like a genuine motivator. What do today's kids learn? No matter what they do, the report to their parents will be positively phrased.

The net result is that you end up writing some reports in the same way that an estate agent describes a dodgy property. It's not 'small', it's 'snug', and Harry is not 'disruptive', he's 'spirited'. Some linguistic gymnastics allow you to write things like, 'Connor has, on one or two occasions, shown that he is capable of focusing on his work for brief periods. In order to improve further, it would be great to see him being less distracted by his peers.'

But wouldn't it be more informative to his parents, and just more direct, if we could write something along the lines of, 'Connor is definitely capable of achieving a B in English, but at the moment his poor behaviour is holding him back.

He spends much of the lesson messing around with his friends rather than concentrating on the task in hand. He needs to urgently turn this around if he is to avoid significant underachievement'?

Comments like this would be the exception, and teachers would have to use their discretion to ensure they weren't puncturing the self-esteem of innocents. But the truth, as I'm sure any sensible parent will agree, is that sometimes kids need their egos massaged and their confidence boosted, and sometimes they need a bit of a kick up the backside. It's part of the art of teaching to know when each is appropriate.

Many schools require teachers to annotate students' work with, 'What went well' and a comment which begins, 'Even better if'. Again, everything has to be positively phrased. And when it comes to grading, I've already mentioned the pressure on teachers to make sure there is a steady upward trajectory in each student's progress.

The reality, of course, is that no learning is entirely linear. It's all about trying something, messing it up and then doing better the next time. You might take a risk on one piece of work; sometimes it will fail and you'll get a low grade, but other times it will pay off and you'll shoot right up. You can't develop by playing it safe – school should be a place where you can feel comfortable trying out different things and inevitably some of those won't work. That's healthy and normal and to be encouraged. I keep coming back to the idea that you go to school not only to learn curriculum subjects, but far more importantly to learn the skills that are going to prepare you for life, and learning how to cope with failure is a pretty important one.

So what's the problem if a graph of a kid's progress is up and down and all over the place? If it were up to me, I would celebrate that rather than call a meeting about it. I wouldn't shy away from telling a child that something they have done hasn't really worked this time. And I would trust teachers to write honest reports which will say what is needed to bring the best out of their students.

One colleague told me recently that they submitted a report which read, 'John is a saint. Regrettably the saint I refer to is St Francis, the patron saint of fools.' It was sent back for him to redo. Maybe that is going too far. But perhaps he wouldn't have been so inclined to troll the system if what he said wasn't so heavily policed.

Keep Your Head Up

One of the trials of being a new teacher is having to endure frequent lesson observations. Everyone from the head teacher to your head of department and a multitude of other hangers-on come along with a clipboard to grade how well you're doing, and you're supposed to continue as though there's nothing out of the ordinary happening, even though the kids can smell your fear and pretty quickly cotton on to the fact that they could easily throw you under the bus.

The worst kind of observations are the ones by Ofsted. The inspectors turn up with little notice every few years (or more often if they feel there's a need), and prowl around the school ducking into lessons here and there, striking fear into the hearts of all they meet. They peer over students' shoulders and look at what they are writing, take their books away to pore over the quality of the marking and, most intimidating of all, they ask the children what you're like as a teacher.

Although almost all inspectors are former teachers, not all have taught recently, and many look as at ease talking to children as a nun in a brothel. One of their favourite opening questions when they crouch down beside a student and try to muster some degree of charm is, 'Could you tell me what it is you're doing?' Of course, when you see this happen, everything in you wills the child to give a coherent explanation of your carefully thought-out lesson. And as sure as the sun rises in the east, each and every time they will choose just about the last student you'd want them to speak to.

A colleague I trained with, a biology teacher, had exactly this experience. She listened with one ear to the boy's reply. 'I'm not totally sure what it is we're doing,' she heard him say. Not a fantastic start. 'But I think it might be science.'

When the news breaks that Ofsted will be visiting us in just one day's time, my mind goes to Sean. With his penchant for putting his head on the desk for large chunks of the lesson, he is not exactly the paragon of engagement they seek. As the class traipse in, I have a quiet word with him. With something approaching desperation I say, 'Sean, I'd love it if you could try to keep your head up today. And you know how much I enjoy hearing your contributions – why not try and put your hand up during one of the discussions.'

He turns his head almost imperceptibly towards me. 'If this is about Ofsted, I'll do you a deal. I'll take my head off the desk if the inspector walks in. And I will put my hand up – my right one if I know the answer and my left one if I don't. But leave me alone the rest of the time.' With time pressing and no real alternative, I accept his dubious offer.

In the event, the inspectors keep a wide berth from my classroom, Sean's head is rarely separated from the desk and I feel as though I have dodged a bullet.

Where the prospect of a visit from Ofsted causes me to resort to striking deals with students, an observation by Liz is something to look forward to. You know that she's on your side, willing you to succeed, but understanding how challenging it is too.

Anything can happen in a classroom, even more so when someone is assessing you. Kids misbehave or faint or cry or fall off their chair or put their hand up to tell you they haven't understood what's been going on for the last half-hour. You forget your resources, or the projector breaks or your pen leaks all over your face.

Liz has an ability to understand the often complex dynamic of a class in minutes but, more than that, no matter what has gone wrong, her feedback will always leave you feeling that you are good at your job and motivated to be even better. She'd never become an Ofsted inspector because she loves classroom teaching too much. But any inspector could learn a thing or two from her.

Royal Appointment

It's nearly the end of the summer term. Ofsted have been and gone and reported that as a school we are 'good', so there is a slightly demob-happy air in the staffroom, where Mary has her audience in the palm of her hand. She has taught at the school for decades, a huge character, loved by children and staff alike. The previous year, a group of her students had nominated her for an MBE for services to education, and she has just collected her award from Windsor Castle, where it was presented by Princess Anne.

'I was so nervous while I was waiting to speak to her,' she says, her voice echoing around the staffroom. All other conversation has stopped anyway because Mary is always worth listening to. She speaks with the authority of a politician, the timing of a stand-up comedian, and the volume of a Cape Canaveral rocket launch.

'I was waiting in line to speak to her, with my fancy hat on and all, and my mouth was totally dry. And then I was in front of her all of a sudden. She asked me, "So why did you become a teacher?" And my mind just went completely blank. There was a silence that felt like it went on and on. I opened my mouth once and nothing came out. Then a second time. And on the third attempt I just heard myself say, in a posh voice, "Well, of course both my parents were teachers." But the whole time I was thinking to myself, "No, they weren't. Neither of them were. My mother was a seamstress and my father was a bus driver." But by that time she had said, "Very good," and moved on. So all I did in my entire conversation with Princess Anne was tell her a lie. My pupils wouldn't believe it!'

The staffroom erupts in appreciation of Mary.

Made It

Not long afterwards, the academic year draws to a close, and our first year as qualified teachers is over. Zoe and I head out to the bars of Cambridge with a few other rookie teachers to celebrate having taught some lessons which were at the very least passable, and having managed to avoid causing lasting damage to any children in the process.

As Aretha Franklin's 'Respect' rings out around the bar we sing along. 'R-E-P-S-E-C-T,' Zoe bellows at the top of her voice. Hold on a second. 'Did you, an English teacher, just misspell the word "respect"?' And then we can't speak any more because the laughter, and the relief of finishing the year, are too much.

We have regularly seen 2 a.m. come and go as we attempted to fill blank lesson plans with sparky ideas. Weekends have become an opportunity to get marking done, and school holidays have evaporated in a blur of admin and reports and emails.

If a kid wrote in their creative writing homework that they'd had a roller coaster of a year, I would note in the margin that they could perhaps think of a more original metaphor. And yet it seems appropriate for the highs and lows of our first year in the classroom.

I've learned that the lows in teaching are deep, dark valleys. When you collect work from a class feeling optimistic and look at it and realise no one has understood you; when you feel you've spent a whole hour trying and failing to get them just to quieten down; when the lesson simply falls apart ... it's not just that it's disappointing or annoying. It feels deeply personal. It feels like a failure. But the highs are like nothing I have ever experienced. Satisfaction isn't even the word. When a child achieves something they didn't think they could it's just magic.

The Difficult Second Year

September appears inexorably over the horizon, and Zoe and I find ourselves walking the corridors again, though with slightly more confidence than we had a year previously, and with both of us managing to stay upright. Junior teachers are entrusted with a form group in their second year. That means that you're responsible for the pastoral care and all-round well-being of around thirty children.

My form are Year 7s, the youngest students in the school. You're the first and last adult they see in their school day, as you register them in the morning and the afternoon. You get to know them as individuals, you get to know their families and I find that you take on the role of advocate for them in their dealings with other teachers. But equally if they have misbehaved elsewhere in the school I tell them that they have let me down, and I actually mean it. Aside from sorting out rows about pencil cases and 'he said, she said' arguments, it is a role I love.

A lesson also appears on my timetable called Personal, Social and Health Education. This is when you meet your form class and are supposed to teach them about everything from revision techniques to drugs, from why they should wear deodorant to how local government works. Hence I find myself projecting a stick man onto the whiteboard, and inviting students to come forward and circle the 'hygiene hot spots'. For every hot spot, we come up with a rule which will help avoid any nasty problems. After circling a stick man's crotch and writing on the board the words, 'Make sure you change your pants every day,' I'd be lying if I said I didn't briefly wonder what I was doing with my life.

Then there's sex education. After a sleepless night I stand in front of a room of expectant faces and opt for the tried and tested, 'Write any questions you have on a piece of paper and pop them into this box. If you don't have any questions, that's fine, just write that on the page and put it in the box too.' The advantage of this approach is that you can ignore any questions which are too personal, pretending that there's no question on that page. And I very quickly learn that, with a group of young people, this is 100 per cent necessary.

The trickiest one asks, 'How hard should you blow when giving a blow job?' It's embarrassing to answer, of course, but it strikes me that it is potentially quite important. So I hear myself, in an out-of-body experience, making the point that you're not trying to inflate anything and that probably 'blow' is something of a misnomer.

But compared to my colleagues with older form groups I have it easy. Some of them are required to demonstrate putting a condom on a large blue plastic penis. These are supplied by the school nurse, and teachers return the model to her pigeonhole afterwards. Passing through the staffroom, my eye is caught by a flash of bright blue. Yes, there is a dildo in the nurse's pigeonhole, with a Post-it note attached to it. On closer inspection it reads, 'Returned with thanks from

Joan.' Joan is an extremely sweet, slightly older teacher. She's been at the school for years.

I see the opportunity and the angel and the devil within me have a very brief battle as to what should be done next. In one quick movement, I take the penis, Post-it note still attached, from the nurse's pigeonhole and put it into my colleague Dan's instead. I'm with him later that day when he goes to check for post. The spectrum of confused faces he pulls is glorious to behold.

Dan's Door Handle

Dan is a colleague in the English department. He's a superb teacher who always believes his students can achieve more than they think they can. He is also a great form tutor. He's got Year 7s this year too, and is determined to train them to be the best form in the school. As part of this mission, he's told them they all need to bring in 'reading books' every day, and be reading in silence by the time he gets to their form room in the morning.

As it's early days he tries to give them a warning that he's nearly there. Some days he takes the outside route so they can see him through the window as he approaches. Sometimes he talks loudly near the room so they can hear him. And today he decides to get down on his hands and knees and rattle the door handle so that they have time to pull their books out. An excellent idea, foiled only by the fact that he has missed an email explaining there would be a room swap with another class this morning. So a senior teacher opens the classroom door to find Dan on his hands and knees zealously rattling the handle. The senior teacher says that his class are working on a project, but they're finding the rattling a tad distracting. Dan mutters some vague apologies, begins to try to explain, but thinks better of it and retreats.

Poetry from Other Cultures

No longer being a new teacher also means being assigned some of the classes the school deems particularly challenging. I have my first bottom set. And a bigger collection of misfits you couldn't imagine. I adore them.

As a teacher you can't have a favourite student. But if I did it would be Kieron. He's fifteen and can barely read or write. What we know of his family background is chaotic and fairly horrendous. His mother had an abusive partner so he was exposed to violence from a young age. He talks slowly and deliberately and somehow has the air of an old man.

We're studying poetry from other cultures, and in particular a lovely poem called 'Search for my Tongue' by Sujata Bhatt. It's about the struggle people can feel when they move from one country to another and are no longer speaking their native language on a daily basis. Before we read it, I ask the class to close their eyes and imagine that they are walking down the street in some foreign city. There are people bustling past them on every side. There are exotic shops and markets all around. Someone stops them in the street and asks them something in a language they don't recognise. They're unable to respond, but the stranger becomes more insistent, repeating what they have said before and demanding an answer.

I tell the class to open their eyes and write down three words to describe how they felt in that scenario. 'I'm not interested in boring words like "bad",' I tell them. 'I want you to show off your vocabulary and demonstrate the brilliant words you know.'

About a minute later I ask whether anyone would be prepared to share the words they have written with the class. Kieron purposefully puts his hand in the air. 'I've written that I would feel distressed.' Long pause. 'And erotic.'

I try to keep the show on the road, despite the fact that the teaching assistant at the back of the room is convulsing with laughter. '"Distressed" is an excellent word, Kieron. I definitely wouldn't change that one at all. Do you ... know what "erotic" means?'

'I've no idea, sir, but you said to use the best words we could think of and that was the best word which came to mind at that moment.'

Vive La France

Liz has asked me if I would accompany her and sixty of the younger pupils, on a week-long trip to France. I jump at the chance. It's not just the opportunity to experience French culture and get to know some of the students a little better outside the school setting, it's the thought of spending time with Liz and learning more about the craft of teaching from one of the best. And, let's face it, having a few days off school doesn't exactly make it a less attractive proposition.

I am to stay with the deputy head of the French partner school that is hosting us, a lady called Ann-Marie. Ann-Marie has a husband and two children in their early twenties. Mr Ann-Marie is a professor of English at the local university and frankly terrifying. Over dinner on the first night he fires the names of various obscure works of English literature at me and seems to take inordinate pleasure in my confessing that, no, I don't think I have read that one as it happens.

As he shows me to my room, he points at a door just across the hallway. 'That's my daughter's room,' he tells me, and he holds my gaze just long enough to communicate the message that he will tear me limb from limb if I think about trying it on with her.

He needn't have worried. As it happens I spent much of the long coach journey wondering what I should do about the fact that I think I'm gay. It's been a recurring thought since I was a teenager myself. Over the years I've railed against it, prayed against it, ignored it, cursed it and even convinced myself that it's a secret I will take to my grave, but I'm starting to wonder whether it's worth revisiting that plan of action. Maybe it's just a result of the extra thinking time you get when you're travelling. Maybe it's being a little older and in the second year of an adult job. Maybe it's seeing increasing numbers of friends partner up and get married. It feels like it's something that's going to have to be addressed.

The kids have a brilliant time in France and behave impeccably. They are marched around assorted chateaux, spend time in school with their French counterparts and have a day in a theme park. Liz leads them with warmth and confidence, sharing their excitement and encouraging them. Every time I speak to Liz I learn more about the real nature of teaching, and I see her look after the children as though they are her own. There's only one kid who is a pain.

Tom won't stop complaining. He's too cold, then he's too hot. He's starving but then he doesn't like any of the food options presented to him. Today he's decided that he has a sore throat. Liz tells him that she will happily take him to the chemist's, but that in France they give medicine for sore throats up the bum. He is miraculously cured. She turns to me and winks.

What a teacher. What a human being.

Text Fail

Jo, one of the other teachers in the English department, lives a few streets away. She is bright and funny and sociable and we occasionally see each other in the evenings. Teachers, by the way, love hanging out with other teachers and talking about teaching. Evenings inevitably start with a promise not to talk about work, and within about fifteen minutes, the conversation has turned to the best text for engaging reluctant readers or the relative benefits of arranging the desks in different ways in the classroom. I texted Jo last night to say she should drop in if she was free and was a bit surprised that I didn't get a response.

Over a school canteen lunch I ask if she wasn't around last night. She looks me in the eye and tells me to check the message I sent her, which I duly do. The message I had intended to send was, 'I'm pretty sure you'll have more exciting plans, but on the off-chance you're free you're welcome to drop in this evening.' Regrettably, due to an unfortunate auto-correct, the message I actually sent read, 'I'm pretty sure I'll have more exciting plans, but on the off-chance you're free you're welcome to drop in this evening.'

I had managed to make it sound as though I thought I was too busy and important to worry about such trivia as whether I would be in for her visit. I also implied that her time is worth so little that she should still call around despite the likelihood she'd be left standing on the doorstep. She graciously accepts my profuse apologies, and I tell myself what I often tell my students – always check your work.

Being A Minor Celebrity

Being out and about in the school catchment area at weekends is an experience. It's probably the closest you can get to being a low-ranking celebrity without selling your soul to some reality TV show. Overwhelmingly I've found kids who see you out of school to be polite and appropriate, albeit agog that you have an existence beyond the school gates and don't live under your desk.

A peculiar thing about working in a big school, though, is that you might know the names of the couple of hundred kids who you teach, and perhaps recognise the faces of a couple of hundred more, but a considerably larger number of them will know who you are. So there can be shouts of 'Hello, sir!' from apparently random groups of teenagers which, if you're out with your friends, can be a source of some amusement.

And they come at all sorts of times you're not expecting them. I have been snoozing on the grass in a park, lying on a trolley giving blood, and walking down a street in mid-town Manhattan when out of the blue someone has shouted, 'Mr Wilson.' Generally these interactions are pretty brief and cordial, but one colleague did draw the line when a parent approached her on a Friday evening in a cinema foyer and asked for advice about helping her daughter with her Shakespeare coursework.

More than once I have been having a very pleasant evening in a pub when a group of sixth form students have walked in and I have apologetically suggested to my very understanding companions that we move on. Supermarkets are particular hot spots because a lot of pupils get part-time or Saturday jobs there. I've become acutely aware of the contents of my trolley, and adept at hiding any booze or other potentially incriminating items under some bags of salad.

And on one occasion I returned from a run, sweaty, panting for air and wearing shorts that were probably too short, to find one of my Year 10s waiting for a bus outside my front door. We looked at each other in mutual horror. She managed to say, 'How was your run?' and I made incoherent gasping noises in response before throwing myself into my flat. I don't know how J-Lo does it.

Year 11 Goodbye

The school year brings with it various set-piece events. In the autumn there is open evening, when prospective parents bring their offspring to gaze upon science experiments and well-choreographed drama productions in a school which is unrecognisably clean. The best-behaved and most pleasant children are invited to act as guides, while polite suggestions are made to the ruffians that this might be an ideal night to catch up on their Xbox activity. Invariably at least one mother asks me whether I am enjoying the sixth form.

Winter means Charities Week, when sixth form students persuade teachers to dress up, dance, sing or otherwise humiliate themselves in the name of good causes. I can't quite remember agreeing to it, but nevertheless I find myself competing in a race around the school grounds on a space hopper. As I watch the film back on a big screen in the assembly hall, I am disappointed to learn that I look ungainly – to put it mildly – bouncing on a rubber ball.

And spring means Year 11 going on their study leave. I've got my last lesson with Sean, Matt and the rest of my ragbag group of characters. I'll miss them. I give them a motivational speech about keeping up the momentum while they're working at home and the importance of finishing strongly. The bell rings and I send them off, wishing them luck. 'We haven't got you a card, sir,' one of them pipes up. 'Cos you're Irish we got you potatoes instead.' And suddenly they are surrounding my desk and throwing down potatoes on which they have scrawled messages of thanks in marker pen. I am equally offended and moved.

In my experience teachers breathe a sigh of relief at this time of year, not because they want to get rid of Year 11, but because their absence edges the workload towards being vaguely manageable. I sometimes think that if I taught only one class of thirty students for their five hours of English per week, I'd be able to plan interesting, engaging, well-paced lessons for them, as well as marking their work in sufficient detail and differentiating their lessons to make sure that the most able are stretched and those who find it hardest are properly supported. I'd make their reports really useful and follow up all issues thoroughly. The reality is that I have six classes of that size. My upbringing was fairly religious and that's helpful because it means I'm used to living with the guilt that I will never be good enough.

Every silver lining, however, has its cloud and Year 11 leaving means that they must have a last day. Schools run on the principles of order and teachers having the authority to enforce that order. But a bunch of sixteen-year-olds who know they never have to darken the door of the building again also know that they have slipped the net and now hold the balance of power.

You can try and threaten to turn them away from their exams if they attempt any stunts that are too audacious, but everyone knows that your words ring hollow, and there is a long tradition of 'muck-up day' pranks. When I was a pupil, I remember washing lines appearing high up in trees in the dead of night, adorned with various items of underwear labelled with teachers' names. The more unlikely it was that a particular member of staff would own a saucy little number, the more certain you could be that their name would be attached to a lacy bra and thong.

Setting off fire alarms is chief among the concerns of management. It might seem like a fairly minor misdemeanour, but when you consider that nearly two thousand children and hundreds of staff are forced to evacuate every time the siren sounds, that is a lot of lost hours. And it's not just the teaching time that evaporates; the catering staff can't get lunch ready, students preparing for exams are adversely affected, and parents who are there to discuss their child being bullied instead find themselves milling around on some tennis courts with a few hundred children, some of whom are the very ones doing the bullying. The remedy for this is that trustworthy pupils from younger year groups are conscripted to guard the fire-alarm points, a task they carry out as diligently as if they had been asked to guard the Crown jewels.

All staff are drafted in to patrol at break and lunchtime, a very low-budget version of shock and awe tactics. But somehow it seems to work this year. There are a few waterbombs, and some pictures of teachers with their heads photoshopped onto various bodies in unsavoury positions are distributed, but that's about it. I find a photo of my head on the body of a leprechaun, and decide, for the second time that day, not to bring up the complexities of thirty years of sectarian conflict in Northern Ireland. The picture could have been a lot worse.

Fads

You might think that the act of communicating an idea to a group of children in such a way that they understand it is a fairly timeless art. Yet what is perceived as good teaching by the powers-that-be seems to change with the direction of the wind. When I first started out in teaching the trend was for 'learning styles': children were either visual, audio or kinaesthetic learners by preference, and any lesson worth its salt would have activities to cater for all three.

So you might incorporate a flow chart on a PowerPoint slide to explain an idea for the visual learners who respond best to what they see, you might plan a peer teaching group session for the auditory learners who prefer listening, and you might try and get them up and role-playing a deleted scene from a play for the kinaesthetic learners who prefer to learn through doing. The value of catering for different learning styles was imparted in our teacher training sessions by our tutors, and in staff meetings by management.

After a couple of years, this pillar of lesson planning, this idea we were led to believe was the be-all and end-all of educational achievement, was quietly forgotten about. Next we were told that a lesson would be a total write-off unless there was an aim on the whiteboard, differentiated for what 'all, most and some' students would achieve.

So you would have an overarching aim for the lesson – 'to be able to explain the ways Shakespeare presents

Othello as a jealous character', for example. Then you would break it down to 'all will be able to identify and discuss events in the text which show Othello's jealousy', 'most will be able to choose and comment on quotations that demonstrate Othello's jealousy' and 'some will be able to analyse the connotations of individual words in the quotations to show how Shakespeare has shown Othello's jealousy'. There were suggestions that you might quietly go around each child and say whether they should be aiming for the 'all', 'most' or 'some' objective. Doing all that for five lessons a day represents a not insignificant amount of time, and it's not clear that it particularly helps.

Then for a while 'teaching' became a dirty word. To stand at the front and proclaim was seen as an indulgent, aggrandising act. The focus was on learning, and learners (for even calling them 'students' or 'children' was to take the focus off learning for too long) must discover things for themselves. Everything would be group challenges and research projects and peer learning. Management announced that we should no longer refer to lesson plans, but should talk about 'learning plans' instead. I remember being told by a more senior teacher that any time I found myself speaking to the class I should ask myself, 'Why?' and stop as soon as possible. References to homework were also banned; it was now 'home learning'. All of this was done with a straight face.

Then there was a change of government, and all of a sudden it was completely fine again for teachers to stand at the front and deliver a lesson. Everything that just a few months before would have had you metaphorically taken out and shot was, more or less overnight, entirely fine, even encouraged. And this whole cycle of changing fashions happened over less than a decade.

The truth, as I think most teachers would tell you, is that there is good in all of these approaches, but none is the elixir you've been waiting for, the long-desired panacea, even though they are often presented as such. It depends on the class you have, the personalities, the topic you're covering and a thousand other variables of which teachers are instinctively aware. Sometimes group work fits the bill. Sometimes it makes sense to explain something at length in a lecture style. Other times you do want to get them up and moving about. My approach, having seen them come and go, is to make a good attempt at each new initiative but treat it with a pinch of salt and accept it's probably not the teaching equivalent of the promised land.

Noodle Head

Dan is regaling the staffroom with a cautionary tale he has acquired from teaching his Year 8s. He was explaining similes to them, and attempting to communicate the idea that you might compare two things which are not the same but which seem similar.

'For example,' he told the class, 'I could say that Sophie's hair is as curly as noodles.'

The class grasped the concept, wrote a few similes of their own and Dan thought no more of this illustration until he got a call from Sophie's parents a few days later. They were complaining that Sophie was very upset because she was now being referred to as 'noodle head' in the playground, and they understood that Dan had 'started it'. Did he, they wanted to know, encourage other children to call Sophie a noodle head?

Sorry is the Hardest Word

I am walking along a corridor when I come across Kieron, the student who would be my favourite if I had favourites, slouched despondently against a wall outside a classroom. I ask him what's wrong.

'Yet again I've been sent out of the room for no reason.'

'Ah, come on, Kieron. I know Mrs Prior very well,' I tell him. 'She is always fair. We both know that she wouldn't send you out for no reason. What really happened?'

'Apparently I kept talking over her.'

'Well, the thing is, Kieron, Mrs Prior has thirty other students in there as well as you. It must be frustrating if you keep interrupting and disturbing everyone else's lesson. Can't you see that's why she sent you out?'

A reluctant, 'I suppose so.'

'Kieron, you're going to have to apologise to Mrs Prior. Do you want to practise by saying your apology to me first, so you have the wording exactly right when you say it to her?'

A shrug. A tut. And eventually, 'Sorry, Mrs Prior. I now realise that there are thirty other students in the class as well as me.' But Kieron hasn't finished yet. 'Though fuck me sideways, you pissed me right off.'

Results Day

Another school year has ended and it's the summer holidays again. The perfect blue sky that lies ahead for the next six weeks has only one cloud on the horizon: my first GCSE results day as a teacher. Sleep in the week before is fretful. My class have definitely all failed. I've accidentally taught them the wrong book, or cocked up the mountain of paperwork you have to fill in for them or maybe I told them all not to write anything in the exam by mistake. In my dream Liz appears in the school hall as children collect their envelopes, shaking her head and saying she's sorry but they have no option but to let me go. She's not angry, she laments, she's just disappointed.

A few hours later, and in the real world, the exams officer hands me the envelope and I reflect on the fact that I am infinitely more nervous than I ever remember being when collecting my own results. As I read down the list it feels as though bricks are being lifted off my shoulders with each result I read. They've passed! And they've mostly passed with better grades than I could have hoped for. Some of them have got As and Bs which are well above what was predicted. Matt got his A, thank God. Only Sean is a disappointment. He got an E, but then he did have his head on his desk for the best part of a year and hand in coursework that he had kept in his trainer, so that's probably not a massive surprise, and he can always re-sit.

They've worked hard on the whole, and for all the mistakes I've made, all the crises of confidence I've had, all the misfired lessons that I've presided over, we got there in the end. After congratulating the kids I head home utterly convinced that no work comes near teaching for job satisfaction.

Plain Old Fanny

September has come round again, and I've been offered some responsibility in the English department. As Key Stage 4 co-ordinator I'll be responsible for helping the head of department to oversee the GCSE course. And almost immediately a problem arises.

Early in the term one teacher goes permanently AWOL with a set of her class's coursework from the previous year in her possession. These assignments count towards the students' GCSE grades at the end of the course. It's unconscionable that these students should suffer because of an issue outside their control. So we have permission from the exam board to redo the coursework orally. In other words, the students will come into a room one by one and we'll ask them some questions on the topic of women in *Far from the Madding Crowd*, which was the original area they studied, and we will award them marks on the basis of their oral responses to those questions. It saves them from rewriting the essays they have already completed.

I am to conduct these interviews with my colleague, Dave. I'd like to put on record that I am not proud of what happened next. But I report it in the interests of full disclosure and in the hope that you will judge me kindly. The first component of this rather unfortunate circumstance is that neither Dave nor I have taught *Far from the Madding Crowd* so are not that familiar with it. In fact we have never read it. But we think that shouldn't stop us from being able to ask a few straightforward questions about the representation of women in the book in this emergency situation.

The students are lined up outside the room. Dave goes out and reminds them that this is an assessed part of their course and they should take it seriously. The first student walks in and takes a seat in front of us. 'Tell us about some of the female characters in *Far from the Madding Crowd* that stand out to you,' Dave says.

'Well, you've got Bathsheba who dresses really ornately,' the student responds, 'and then you've just got plain old Fanny, ain't ya?'

Dave laughs first, a short grunt that could be mistaken by an unaccustomed ear for a cough. My mouth makes some kind of squawk and Dave follows up with a laugh-wheeze that sounds like Muttley on fifty a day. Dave pretends to get something out of his bag underneath the table. I turn in my chair and face the back wall.

I am fully aware that this sort of behaviour from two grown men is appalling. But it's like getting the giggles at a funeral: the more inappropriate it is, the more utterly irrepressible the laughter becomes. We do everything we can to reassure the child that she has done nothing wrong, and she ended up with a good mark. She covered herself in considerably more glory than the supposed adults in the room.

Bad News

One grey Monday morning, the head calls a special staff meeting. The hall is abuzz with speculation. Are Ofsted coming back? Is the head leaving? Are there going to be redundancies? The truth is worse than any of those things. Liz, wonderful Liz, who mentored and looked after us as teachers just starting out, who picked up the pieces when everything went wrong, who sang our praises and fought our corner when we needed it, who is the best teacher many of us know and who always has that naughty twinkle in her eye, has been diagnosed with cancer. It's the same illness which claimed her sister, and the prognosis is not good. She is going to carry on teaching for as long as she can, because she loves it so much. It's cruel beyond words, and everyone in the room is heartbroken.

The Power of Praise

Three years since I first entered a classroom as a trainee teacher and I feel like I've learned, through trial and brutal error, and not least through Liz, one of the most important lessons of teaching teenagers. Your greatest tool is not your books, not your fancy projector, nor your cleverly thought-out starter activity. The absolute number one thing is your relationship with the students in front of you. It's what they think of you, and even more important, how they perceive you think of them.

I've already mentioned that this doesn't mean being matey with students. Neither does it mean you must shout and bellow in an effort to exert your authority.

In fact it might be worth diverging briefly on the role of shouting in the classroom. I have seen teachers do it hugely ineffectually. I have done it hugely ineffectually myself. The first few times were when I was truly frustrated with a child's behaviour. I realised pretty early on that it was a bad idea to ever shout from a place of genuine anger or frustration; students sense that they have you rattled and you've lost control, and it's difficult to communicate clearly when your emotions are heightened because you're more likely to say something you regret. I resolved that next time I shouted it would be an act, a tactic to be deployed in certain circumstances when it might help underline a point.

I've met many teachers who hold that there is no place for shouting in the classroom but I don't agree. Used sparingly and thoughtfully I've seen it be devastatingly effective. I suppose it's a matter of personal style.

But regardless of whether you ever shout or not, at the very centre of how you deal with students, there must be honest praise. It was teaching a few so-called low-ability sets that brought this home for me. The students arrive at their English lesson believing they can't do English. They've had years of low scores – literally a decade, in many cases – of feeling disheartened and discouraged about the subject. And for many it's not just English – they feel they're not cut out for school or study of any kind. They journey from lesson to lesson, their self-esteem taking a further battering with each classroom they pass through.

I was lucky at school to be reasonably academic. I found exams straightforward on the whole. I remember even enjoying some; they were a chance to show off and when the papers were handed back, there was usually praise from the teacher. Of course you're going to enjoy people saying nice things about your performance.

PE, however, was a different matter. Hand–eye coordination has never been my strong suit, and I vividly recollect the fear of a hockey ball coming in my direction, or the sense of dread I'd feel all day knowing that I would have to go out on a rugby pitch in the afternoon. I also remember the humili-ation when I inevitably dropped the ball or missed the pass. I can still hear the PE teacher's voice in my head berating me and remember the misery it caused.

But that was only an hour or two a week. I sometimes imagine what it would have been like if the school system had valued physical prowess over academic ability. I would have been in a bottom set, no question about it. The constant criticism and public failure would have ground me down. It was bad enough as it was; being good at sport at school was so tied up with status and masculinity and credibility. The trauma of constant failure was real.

But if the whole education set-up was built around it, I would undoubtedly look for any way at all I could skive lessons. Teachers would be the enemy. The last thing I would want to do would be to cooperate with them. And this response would have been deeply ingrained over years and years, since I was four or five.

I try and remember that sense of alienation when new groups of students arrive in my classroom. It's why when I ask a question and a kid comes up with a response which is interesting or shows they've been thinking or is even just slightly better than what they would normally come out with, it's such a pleasure to praise them and watch their reaction. On occasion I will stop the whole lesson and say, 'Anna, that is a really, really brilliant point. I hadn't thought of that character in that way before. Thank you for putting your hand up.'

Their reaction is often dramatic and instant. Sometimes you can almost see their shoulders go back, and watch them sit a little taller and straighter in their chairs. And it's a gift which keeps on giving, because they generally can't wait to contribute again, and then again. Like shouting, it needs to be used sparingly; overuse ruins its effect and it needs to be genuine; kids can smell insincerity a mile off. It doesn't solve deeply ingrained literacy problems at a stroke. But it certainly improves your relationship with them, and makes them more open to what you have to say. And that's half the battle.

Middle Leadership in Action

Based on pretty much nothing the school has suggested that I participate in a leadership programme. The course is called 'Middle Leadership in Action', and it's aimed at encouraging more teachers to make the move to middle management. I hate it.

For starters it seems to have been lifted directly from a business management course. It's literally as though someone has done a 'find and replace' search on Microsoft Word and changed 'business' to 'school'. But schools aren't businesses, children aren't clients, these are not institutions intended to generate profit. There is next to nothing in it about kids or lessons or exams or classrooms, and as a result it feels about as far away from useful and practical as it's possible to be.

Instead it is laden with the worst sort of management speak. We do a half-day session on the topic of 'blockers'. Blockers, apparently, are people who get in the way of you doing what you want to do as a leader. The people who put their hand up in the meeting and question your plans, or who gossip about your ideas behind your back and try to turn the team against you, or who just refuse to cooperate with whatever it is you want them to do. 'We're going to brainstorm the ways you can deal with blockers, so you can get on with the plans you want to introduce,' the facilitator announces. 'How would you deal with a blocker?'

I can't help it. My hand is instantly up. 'Surely though it depends on the circumstances? Like whether they're blocking what you're doing maliciously or because they have genuine concerns that are worth talking about.'

'We're talking about how you would remove a blocker who is stopping you doing what you want to do with your team,' comes the response, through teeth that are already gritted. There is no room in their script for views that are remotely nuanced. The suggestions which make it onto the flipchart include launching formal disciplinary procedures against them, killing them with kindness and being sure to enquire how their children are doing so as to improve your rapport with them.

'Yeah but ...' I interrupt, 'isn't it also important to consider that sometimes they might not actually be a blocker? They might be someone who has got sincere concerns about your plans, and sometimes they might even be right. Maybe we should listen to their views and if necessary admit that we were wrong?'

It's as if I had just announced that I would like to ritually sacrifice a goat in the middle of the room and smear its blood over the faces of the facilitators. They look at me with mirthless smiles and explain again that it is an important part of management to be able to deal effectively with blockers. I am sitting beside a friend from my school who tells me that I shouldn't put up my hand again. I have become a blocker.

Then there's the teaching itself. The people leading the sessions are teaching teachers. They're teaching teachers to lead teams of teachers. And yet the standard of their own teaching is laughable. In the last session of the course we are each given a balloon. They tell us to inflate the balloon, and then use a marker pen to write our biggest fears and anxieties about becoming a leader onto it.

It doesn't take Psychic Sally to deduce that we are going to have a ceremonial and cringe-inducing popping of the balloons to correspond with us putting our fears behind us and stepping up to the challenges of leadership. That would have been terrible, but at least that would have made sense. What actually happens is even worse: they're just ignored. The balloons sit on our tables and are never referred to again. I mean ... why didn't we just write those fears on Post-it notes instead of BALLOONS? Come to that, why did we write them down at all?

As if these tortuous sessions, which needless to say the school has paid handsomely for, aren't enough, in between them we are supposed to complete homework. As teachers, we obviously set homework every day. But try getting a teacher to do it and you are on to a loser. Especially when the home-work consists of reading largely irrelevant articles and completing patronising online modules.

The guy in charge tells us that he receives stats that show how long we have spent on the online tasks. When it comes to presenting the certificates at the end of the last session, he says that for many of us it will be a hollow success because we haven't committed the time necessary to make real improvements. That may be true, but at least we got a free balloon.

Night Classes

It's not only at the Middle Leadership in Action sessions that getting teachers to do their homework is nigh on impossible. I've enrolled in Spanish night classes at a sixth form college near my flat in a bid to rekindle the dying embers of my A level Spanish. They start at seven on Wednesday evenings, so I'm often dashing there more or less direct from school. And I've noticed something odd happening.

At the night classes I appear to regress to being a stroppy Year 10 boy. I seem to do all the things that frustrate me in students. I quite often turn up without a pen. When I am asked where my homework is I shrug and mutter something about having been very busy. I find myself staring out the window when I'm supposed to be reading about the Spanish train network.

It's a phenomenon I've noticed in staff meetings at school too. Some teachers rush for the back row. They pass notes between each other. And quite often they have whispered chats while the head is speaking. I'm sure there's some deep psychological explanation for why some of us display the behaviour we spend our days trying to quash. Whatever it is, teachers don't always make an easy audience.

An Important Note

Year 8 are sitting exams. I am at the front of the room while they feverishly scrawl down their responses to some questions about war poems. There is a knock on the door. I beckon a girl with pigtails to come in.

'Excuse me, Mr Wilson, but I have a very important note from Miss Cavendish.' The note is written on a piece of A4 paper and it is stapled around the outside. I tear the staples open and unfold the note. It's Zoe's unmistakably perfect handwriting and it reads, 'Are you as bored of these Year 8 assessments as I am?'

I can absolutely picture the mischievous look on Zoe's face as she handed the note to the child. 'Please tell Miss Cavendish the answer is, "Yes, definitely".'

American Exchange

Caroline from the maths department seems to have forgotten that I once told her that her son liked a bit of incest, because she has sent me an email asking if I would like to go for a coffee and talk about an exciting project. For years now the school has run an exchange programme with a school in Chicago. The teachers who led it have decided they've done it for long enough, so Caroline wants to know whether I might be up for taking charge of it with her. She hasn't even finished her sentence before I say yes.

I took part in Spanish exchanges when I was at school, and look back on them as important life experiences. Nothing really felt daunting to me after living for two weeks with a family based an hour outside of Barcelona, especially when the only things I could say to them were, 'Yes,' 'I am quite tall and have blond hair,' and, 'Please may I have a one-way ticket to York.' There may not be the same language barrier for an American exchange, but I jump at the idea of giving kids brought up in rural Essex the chance to experience life in inner-city Chicago. There is a lot of talk about resilience in education, and how we can foster it. As far as I'm concerned, there aren't many better ways than an exchange.

We set about recruiting twenty-five sixteen- and seventeen-year-olds to take part, as do our American counterparts. Apparently tradition has it that the Brits are responsible for doing the matchmaking of who will stay with whom, so one evening Caroline invites me round to her house and we set about trying to put them together into pairs.

We have asked our lot to write a description of their hobbies and interests, and the Americans have done the same. We have to work within all sorts of constraints like not putting people who have allergies to pets in homes where there are four dogs, and trying to put vegetarians together if feasible, but beyond that we aim to match students with broadly similar interests. The problem is that we keep getting as far as pair 24 and high-fiving each other at how well we are doing, and then discover that our only remaining two are a four-foot, shy, vegan British girl with an interest in horses and a six-foot-five American basketball player who exists on burgers and enjoys cage fighting, and we have to go back to the drawing board again.

We debate long and hard, ironically over a glass of wine, about what rules we should put in place for our kids on the trip, with a particular focus on alcohol. Caroline and I both know that some other trips turn a blind eye to older kids drinking moderately abroad, and there is the argument that it's better they do it under adult supervision rather than sneaking off and getting into trouble. But I am pretty adamant that we should take a hard line. They are underage for buying booze in the UK, never mind the US. And if we are in any way soft and they end up getting injured or worse … it just doesn't bear thinking about.

So I write a contract that includes the line, 'I agree that if I am found to have consumed any alcohol at all I will immediately be sent home at the expense of my family. If this happens on the British leg of the exchange I will forfeit my trip to America without refund,' and I insist that pupils and parents sign it. I'm not sure we will actually enforce this policy in its entirety and ship people home, but it feels better to have that in writing and then we can row back from it if necessary. I suspect it focuses the minds of a few parents too, in the pre-trip chats they have with their offspring.

Pairs eventually matched and behaviour contracts in place, we set about planning an itinerary for twenty-five American teenagers who are due to arrive in a few weeks' time.

Food Fight

The talk of the staffroom is a horror story that unfolded at break time. There were, as usual, three or four staff on duty in the canteen. And, as usual, it was packed with students queuing to buy drinks and sandwiches, and all the tables were occupied with groups of friends from different years. It's not even really clear who started it, but someone, somewhere, threw a sausage roll at another table. Retaliation came in the form of a cream bun, and in no time the whole thing had escalated to a vision from your nightmares.

Kids who have never so much as handed homework in a day late are caught up in it, launching their yoghurts across the room with the best of them. The staff stand on the sidelines shouting hopelessly, 'This must stop at once,' but no one hears and no one complies. Missiles are raining down now, there is barely a child not covered with assorted foodstuffs and the noise levels are quickly moving off the scale. One teacher ducks out to call the cavalry, and before long the whole senior leadership team are staring on in disbelief, treading that fine line between trying to assert their authority whilst avoiding the ignominy of taking a sandwich to the face. The bell rings for the start of the next lesson and a human mass of children file out of the canteen doors, with the odd pizza slice sailing over their heads for good measure.

Mercifully I have been on duty on the other side of the school, and only see the aftermath as I walk back to my classroom. It often strikes me how schools are microcosms for society as a whole, sharing many of the same challenges. As I survey the fries sliding down the walls and the soft drinks pooling in fizzy puddles on the floor, I am reminded that order in schools is dependent on students forgetting how substantially they outnumber staff. In schools, as in society, the veneer of civilisation that keeps the whole show on the road is remarkably thin.

Lunchtime Scrap

A colleague in the staffroom is talking about Kieron. About ten minutes into his lesson, Kieron had put his hand up and asked an unusual question: 'Can I send myself out of the class?'

This colleague had hesitated before responding; it's not unusual for Kieron to be sent out for poor behaviour, but for him to request to be sent out ... this is a first. 'Okay,' the teacher cautiously responds.

He leaves Kieron loitering outside the door for a couple of minutes before popping out to try to ascertain what on earth is going on. Kieron is ready to talk.

'The thing is, sir,' he begins, 'I got in a bit of a scrap at lunchtime. My trousers got ripped. And my boxers got ripped. And one of my balls is hanging out.' My colleague's eye is drawn automatically downwards and he is able to confirm that, yes, there is a gaping hole in Kieron's trousers and a testicle is indeed peeping out to say good afternoon to the world. 'I am not going back in that room while there is a chance that a girl could see my ball,' is Kieron's final word on the matter.

After some head-scratching and toing and froing, the teacher comes up with a plan. Kieron will go and see his head of year at break time and she will provide a spare pair of trousers as well as investigating whatever caused this unfortunate rip. In the meantime Kieron agrees to come back to the lesson but only with the aid of an A level physics textbook which he will hold over his crotch. Scuttling sideways like a crab, and with a double-page spread on electronic circuits preserving his modesty, Kieron takes his seat again and another diplomatic incident is averted.

WKD Blue

I have been offered a small promotion to assistant director of sixth form which means that my English teaching timetable is reduced and I take pastoral responsibility for a hundred or so sixteen- to eighteen-year-olds in the sixth form. They are bright, engaged, motivated and have their lives ahead of them. It's a joy.

Every ointment must have a fly, however, and the bluebottle threatening my happiness is the horror of having to organise the sixth form ball. I need hardly tell you how big a deal this is when you're a teenager; it is the sole topic of conversation in the common room and around the corridors for about six months ahead of the event. I imagine that the local branch of Moss Bros would cease to exist were it not for the stream of awkward boys passing through its doors for their very first suit fitting.

It occurs to me that I never considered when attending my own end-of-school party that it might be even slightly stressful for the teachers concerned. Now I am able to think of little else. There's just so much that could go wrong. There are a few hundred students, all of whom are entitled to bring a partner, some of whom will be from outside the school and a few of whom could be my age or older. And as it's a school function we're meant to ensure there'll be no booze.

The first challenge arises when a worried mother phones me at school a few weeks before the big day. She explains that she's a bit concerned about her son. He hasn't been able to find a date to bring to the ball. She says that she knows I'm busy but is there any possibility at all that I might be able to approach a few nice girls on his behalf and see if any of them would go with him. I explain as politely as I can manage that sadly we can't extend the service we provide to arranging dates.

The day itself dawns. The ball committee has decided on a nautical theme and the kids are arriving in their finery. We've set up a team of staff to search them for alcohol as they go in. It turns out that it's quite hard to stop a few hundred teenagers getting their hands on alcohol. Some have hidden it under their hats. Some have it down their trousers. We find hipflasks and bottles and cartons and cans secreted in all manner of places. Some particularly resourceful students have visited the hotel in advance, and buried bottles in the garden. When we find their stash, I feel like I've smashed a major drugs ring. As a result of our contraband seizures, I am drinking WKD Blue with my dinner for weeks afterwards.

The only other slight hiccup occurs when a couple, the only male same-sex couple at the event, get a little too passionate outside. The head of PE goes to pour metaphorical cold water over them. Although given that he's dressed as a sailor, they might be more amused than chastened.

As I lie in bed reflecting on how the night went, trying to ignore the thump of late-noughties dance music lingering in my ears, I am in awe of that same-sex couple who were so comfortable in their own skins that they were prepared to go to a social event with all their peers. They seem to have no angst or shame or guilt. That, to me, is remarkable.

Good Reception

It takes a lot more than just teachers to run a school. There is a small but dedicated army of teaching assistants, who make school tolerable, and even enjoyable, for dozens of students who would otherwise have dropped out of the system, and who do their job for next to no money. There are dinner ladies and gents, and maintenance staff and office staff, and there are not enough of any of them to do all the work they're expected to do, but they get on with it anyway. And then there are the receptionists. Receptionists have an impact on a school which reaches far beyond the desk they occupy by the front door.

I have worked with one or two who didn't want to be there. They disliked teenagers and didn't seem to know how to talk to them. They resented the ever-ringing phone and one judged a message from Ofsted about an imminent inspection as not important enough to pass on.

But most receptionists are worth their weight in gold. They are the glue that holds the dilapidated buildings together. They are equally adept at comforting anxious children, stopping kids from kicking footballs down the corridor and de-escalating parents who turn up at reception baying for a particular teacher's blood. They are a picture of discretion in how they deal with even the most confidential information, and they stay cheerful even when *everyone* who passes them in the corridor wants to stop for a chat. Schools are well advised to choose their receptionists properly and teachers are well advised to treat them with respect.

The Americans are Coming

Caroline and I set off for Heathrow to meet our cousins from across the pond, and accompany them back to school where they will be matched up with their host families. A few days beforehand we had a panic about how we would find them in the crowded arrivals hall, so Caroline's daughter was drafted in to create a couple of enormous banners so that we could be seen above the throng. The only issue when we arrive is that we are the only other humans there, save a couple of older guys holding taxi signs. So we stand in a deserted arrivals area, holding aloft an entirely unnecessary banner like a couple of lemons. Even the outgoing and confident Americans look a little embarrassed for us when they arrive.

As we pull into the school, our kids are clapping and cheering the arrival of their partners, and I hear one American say, 'It's like Facebook has come to life.' There is much whooping and hugging (the Americans) and saying, 'Nice to meet you,' and firm handshakes (the Brits).

Over the next few days we take them to Warwick Castle and Thorpe Park, and they go on an overnight trip to Edinburgh, but the jewel in the crown of their time in the UK is to be a private tour of the Houses of Parliament, which I have arranged through our local MP. It's brilliant. They get to walk through the House of Commons and the House of Lords, trace the route the Queen takes at State Openings and see the view of the London Eye from the riverside bars. At the end of the session the MP, a kindly older man, has arranged a Q&A. This is where things begin to go a little wrong.

Our visitors have picked up various bits of British news, including a few fairly garbled facts about the parliamentary expenses scandal. A nugget which seems to have lodged in one girl's head is the fact that the former Home Secretary Jacqui Smith had to pay back some money that her husband had spent on renting an adult movie.

When she comes to ask her question, to a man entirely unconnected from that escapade and with a blameless expense record, it sounds like this: 'How come you spent money on porn?' A shocked intake of breath from all in the room, not least the MP. Sensing the slightly hostile reaction, the girl starts digging and it's not long before the hole she is in threatens to consume her. 'No! Don't try to deny it! You did! Why do you think it's perfectly acceptable to hire a porno and watch it at home when your wife doesn't know? Why would you do that?'

The MP very politely explains that the girl may have got a few wires crossed, and we retreat before we cause any more diplomatic incidents.

The visit comes to a close with a dinner in Cambridge for all the students and staff involved in the exchange. The head teacher and his wife are to attend, along with Caroline and me and the American teachers. I haven't had much cause to chat with the head and have never met Mrs Head, and I am to sit beside her at the dinner which is a slightly nerve-wracking prospect. Caroline and I brainstorm all the possible topics of conversation I could bring up so I can feel prepared when we meet.

'Ryan, may I introduce my wife?' the head says, gesticulating towards her.

'Lovely to meet you,' I say, extending my hand.

So far, so good. Unfortunately, however, Mrs Head goes for air kisses and my outstretched hand gets caught in the crossfire, ending up unceremoniously resting on her breast for what I can only describe as an uncomfortably long amount of time. My only consolation is that I managed not to question her about her porn-viewing habits.

Liz's Cancer

I bump into Liz in the corridor. She looks as she always does, serene, happy to be in school and as though there is no one she would rather see. I don't really know what to say to her about her diagnosis and, after a bit of small talk about marking and holidays, tell her as much. Her emotional intelligence is so honed, her ability to put people at their ease so great, that she handles even my extreme awkwardness effortlessly. She tells me that she feels well enough although she gets tired easily. She feels bad about missing lessons when she is away getting treatment. And she is on her way to photocopy some things for a new game she has devised for her Year 8s to help them learn their French verbs.

And then she asks all about how I'm getting on, how I'm finding the job, whether I've had any more run-ins with the police, which kid is doing my head in the most. Every answer I gives feels like it couldn't matter less compared to what she is going through. And yet she listens and sympathises and agrees and laughs. As we reach the end of the corridor and head our different ways, I find myself gently shaking my head, in awe at this remarkable human being.

Out of the Closet

It's a couple of weeks later, on a balmy Friday evening, that I'm sitting in Zoe's living room and we're making our way through a bag of kettle chips. We're reliving the highs and lows of the week. Zoe has had a thirteen-year-old boy write an epic four-page love poem dedicated to her, in which he compared her hair to butter. She gives a dramatic reading of the lines in question.

I should be finding this hilarious but I'm oddly quiet. Zoe doesn't know it but my mouth is dry and my heart feels as though it could puncture my shirt at any moment. 'There's something I need to tell you.' The words tumble out quickly before I have the chance to stop them. 'I think I might be gay.'

It's a moment I had rehearsed over and over; the first time I have said the words out loud. At one point in my life I thought it was a phrase I would never utter. Rural Northern Ireland was a wonderful, beautiful place to grow up but, as far as I knew, there simply weren't any other gay people. I didn't have friends who were gay, the word was never mentioned in any lessons, it wasn't featured in any books I read. The only times homosexuality was ever referred to were in the playground ('Don't want to play football? Don't be gay!' 'You've actually done that homework? You massive gay!') and occasionally from the pulpit where it was spoken of in sermons in hushed tones as one of the scourges of society. I remember lying in bed when I was thirteen or fourteen, and just thinking, 'I will have to keep this a secret for the rest of my life.'

I had actually booked in to see a counsellor a few weeks before speaking to Zoe. Since I started teaching I had watched and been inspired by the confidence with which some teenagers were able to embrace their identities. And it felt as though the world was starting to change, and at a pace. The sort of sleights that were routinely overlooked when I was at school were increasingly not tolerated in educational settings. It felt like the right time to take the first nervous, fledgling steps towards dealing with the issue which I had kept on the back burner for so long.

In the first session I couldn't even tell the counsellor what the problem was. It took a couple of hours of her patient encouragement before I could say those words to her, and she smiled and said, 'That's great.' She told me later that my whole posture changed in that same instant – my shoulders lowered, my legs stopped their impatient tapping and my whole face relaxed.

There's a pause. It's momentary, but in my head it's a fortnight. Then Zoe is smiling and hugging me and we're both crying. 'I think what put me off the scent is that you dress like that,' she says, in a cruel slight on my ill-fitting jeans and a T-shirt that is entering its second decade of service. 'We are going shopping,' she says. I tell her that her hair does indeed look a bit buttery.

Face

One of the good things about having done the job for a few years is that, by the third or fourth time you come to teach something, you generally know what works and what doesn't. That's the case with the novel I'm doing with Year 8. It's called *Face* and it's written by Benjamin Zephaniah. It's a great book about a child who has a facial disfigurement, and how he deals with the various prejudices people exhibit when they first meet him.

There's an activity I have done a few times now which involves getting the class to find examples of various types of language in a particular chapter: accent, dialect, formal language, exclamations and taboo language. In this chapter, the boy with the disfigurement gloriously tells some of his aggressors to 'piss off'. Year 8 kids, as you can imagine, adore this particular language usage.

We recap again what the word 'taboo' means and I ask the class whether anyone is able to find an example of taboo language in this chapter. It's usually one of the confident, slightly cheeky boys that sticks their hand up and triumphantly shouts the words, 'Piss off.' And every year my reaction is the same. With all the theatricality I can summon, I turn dramatically towards the child in question and roar, 'WHHAAAAT did you just say to me?'

If it has worked well, a stunned silence will fall over the room. The boy in question will open and close his mouth a

few times in an attempt to explain. I will leave him in a state
of panic for about two seconds, before breaking into a smile
and telling him I'm joking and that he is completely right. It's
a very small thing. But every year I really look forward to
that lesson.

Just My Nightie

I have fortnightly meetings with my line manager Kathy. She has responsibility for discipline throughout the school, and I am convinced that no one could do the job better. Her reputation for taking no nonsense means that kids, and more than a few staff, find her scary but that is precisely what makes her so suited to her role.

During one of our meetings I notice that she has left her sizeable bunch of keys in the lock on the outside of her office door. I point it out, making some comment about how a kid with a grudge could easily lock her in. She tells me with a grin that it's a trust exercise. She knows that no one would ever dare do it, and she wants to communicate to any potential miscreant that she knows they're too scared. That, I reflect, is a genius power move.

One day Kathy tells me that straight after our meeting she has a boy coming to see her who she suspects of daubing graffiti on the school bus. The boy is one of the school's few actual tough characters. She's had several independent witnesses tell her that he's the one responsible, but given the control the boy exercises over his peers, they're all terrified about speaking on the record. She needs to get him to confess. She asks if I want to watch how she approaches it. Of course I do.

She has the boy sit on a chair in the middle of her office. She asks him if he knows anything about the graffiti on the school bus. He grins, looks around the room and happily replies that he has no idea what she is talking about. What happens over the next ten minutes is a masterclass in interrogation to rival that which any chief inspector in the country could give.

Kathy picks holes in his story. She is by degrees so quiet she is almost whispering and then raises her voice to emphasise a particular inconsistency in his account. She's walking around him, describing the inconvenience for the bus driver who was forced to spend his evening clearing graffiti off the bus rather than having an evening with his children. She's invoking the boy's mother, reminding him how disappointed she would be if he made things worse by continuing to lie. In front of my eyes over those ten minutes the boy's cockiness melts away and he is confessing that he was responsible for the graffiti, he's apologising and promising never to do it again. I am in awe of how Kathy has wrung this information out of him. Every school needs someone like her.

In the staffroom, however, and in our meetings, Kathy is as kind and supportive a senior colleague as you could hope for. And she's funny. When I tell her about how Zoe and I got lost on the way to work and had to face our Year 11 classes she sympathises and tells me a story from her early career which she says still haunts her.

She had been teaching history to a particularly unruly group of Year 9s. What they had done wrong is lost in the mists of time but whatever it was it had necessitated Kathy giving them one of her famous dressings-down. She was in full flow when she became aware of something moving on her body. She ignored it as best she could and continued with the telling-off, but before long something fell out the bottom of her dress and landed on the floor.

On this particular day she had been getting dressed in the dark as her husband was starting work later. It slowly dawned on her that she hadn't taken her nightie off properly, and that it had just dropped to the ground in front of a class of thirty teenagers.

In a sign of quite how unflappable she is, Kathy still didn't break her stride in addressing the class. Instead she picked the garment up with her toe, grabbed it with one hand and put it to one side. Some plucky, foolhardy kid had the temerity to ask, 'Miss, what was that?'

Kathy said she summoned all the nonchalance she could muster, and replied, 'That? That's just my nightie,' before finishing the tirade. Now that is class.

Chicago

It's early in the morning and we're on a coach heading for the airport and the return leg of the Chicago exchange. I take the opportunity to remind the group about the importance of looking after their passports as they go through the airport. I think I might have used the phrase, 'You're all more or less adults – we are trusting you to be responsible.'

When, therefore, a nice man taps me on the shoulder on the way to the gate to say, 'Er, I think you dropped your passport,' you'll understand that my first instinct wasn't to thank him but to hope that none of our group had noticed this interaction. Safe to say that they had noticed it, all of them, and I was treated to an extended round of applause.

My exchange partner is Tom, an English teacher at the Chicago school. He and his wife Sandy are great hosts, and Caroline and I spend the time that we are not with the kids in a blur of social engagements with the staff there. When Tom and Sandy ask me if I have any news, I cautiously tell them that I have come out of the closet. They couldn't be more delighted. I think they had seen through my previous rather lacklustre attempts to claim that the right girl just hadn't come along yet, and I find their positivity really touching.

A couple of days later they announce that they've arranged for me to have coffee with their football coach. When he came out as gay a few years ago, it sent ripples through the system

– the football coach being a god amongst men in an American high school.

Todd – of course his name is Todd – and I sit across from each other a few days later and he tells me about his fears before he came out: ridicule, loss of authority, even losing his job. Yet, overwhelmingly, he says he found even the football community to be supportive and uplifting. And he gives me some brilliant advice which has stayed with me to this day.

'If and when people struggle to accept your sexuality,' he says, 'be patient with them. There's an impulse to lash out, to tell them that this is the way it is and they'll just have to get used to it. But it's often better to play a longer game, and to try to see where they're coming from so that you can reassure them as necessary. Try and understand,' he went on, 'that they will sometimes be grieving for the life they saw for you. And that you chose the moment when you were ready to come out, but they have not always had time to get used to the idea.'

I know some people in the LGBT+ community will see that as unduly apathetic, and there are definitely circumstances in which it is right to bring the fight. But I think there is considerable wisdom in what he said.

The whole exchange goes brilliantly with a packed itinerary of trips and tours for the students. I ask the kids to write a few words about what the exchange has meant to them. Quite a few say they have made friends for life. Many pairs have already planned to meet up off their own bat in the summer holidays. And almost all mention the benefits of being immersed in a culture so different from that of rural Essex. It's been a massively enriching experience for everyone and I very much count myself in that number.

Work Experience

The spring term every year brings with it Year 10 work experience placements. They go off to a local barber or estate agent or supermarket for a fortnight and learn the essentials of the world of work, and they return to school reinvigorated, with a clear vision of where their life is going and why study matters and they are never distracted from their schoolwork again. Or, to give a less varnished version of what sometimes happens, they go and sit around for hours on end in a place where there isn't much to do, getting in everyone's hair, while teachers celebrate having two weeks of relative peace.

Of course, neither vision is entirely fair. Some pupils plan their placements really carefully, and get a lot out of them. Others go somewhere that they end up detesting, and that's as useful a lesson as any. But there are always some who don't start thinking about it until too late and end up being allocated whatever placement is left on the shelf.

Regrettably teachers aren't allowed to loll around in the staffroom while the kids are off dipping their toes into the working world. You're required to go and visit some of your class in their workplaces in the time you have gained. Plan it right and you can see behind the scenes in some really interesting places, as well as getting to know the kids you teach in a different environment.

I have never seen teachers move more quickly than when the email goes around that the work experience visit sign-up sheet has gone up in the staffroom. Today is that day. Dan and I get there so fast, the drawing pin must surely still bear the heat of the thumb that had pushed it into the noticeboard. We scan the possibilities as quickly as we can, and both our eyes are drawn to a particularly pleasant pub in the next town. The only issue is that the student who is spending his placement there, Dane, isn't known to either of us. Also it's meant to be one teacher visiting one pupil. But ... if we can somehow both sign up and hope no one notices that neither of us has ever taught Dane, we could legitimately spend an afternoon in a pub during work.

We decide to brazen it out, both scrawl our initials beside Dane's name and, miraculously, no one questions it. We rock up at the pub on a sunny Thursday afternoon and tell the jolly landlord that we're here to visit Dane, the guy on work experience. He says we should have a seat, and we are glad to accept his offer, unable to believe our luck that we are here rather than stuck in school.

'Dane, your teachers are here!' we hear the landlord shout.

Dane comes out and looks around the pub before uttering five words which expose our wrongdoing in its entirety: 'Which ones are my teachers?'

Act 3 Scene 2

This year's upper sixth class pose a particular challenge. They're perfectly pleasant, they work hard and they're pleasingly engaged with gothic literature. The problem is Amelia. She's just too good. She's much more widely read than me and a great deal more confident in expressing her opinions. I am teaching someone who is simply better at my subject than I am. Dan taught her for GCSE and wrote at the end of one of her essays that she needed to find a publisher rather than a teacher.

I find myself looking at her to check that she's making notes on what I'm saying, because if Amelia is writing it down it must be good stuff. I am seeking the approval of a teenager!

She puts her hand up during a lesson on duality in *Frankenstein*. 'Sir, do you think there are some echoes here of *The Tempest* Act 3 scene 2?'

'Mmmm,' I say, buying myself some time while I try to recall exactly what happens in *The Tempest*, never mind Act 3 scene 2. What I should have said is, 'That's so interesting. The honest answer is I don't know. But why don't we both look into it? Maybe we can have a chat one lunchtime next week and you could give the class a little presentation on the similarities.' But my own insecurity overwhelms me and I say instead, 'Maybe. But that's not a point I'd want to push too far, to be honest. It's a bit tenuous.'

The Teacher's Teacher

As autumn becomes winter, Liz passes away. She continued teaching right up to a few weeks before the end, and what a tribute that is to her, to her steeliness, to her resilience and to her love for teaching. She was an extraordinary teacher, an exemplar, a role model for anyone who knew her.

She was also a teacher in the broadest sense of that word. She taught French and German, brilliantly, and her students adored her. She taught us fledgling teachers how to survive and thrive in the profession. But more importantly she taught us all, staff and students alike, about patience and humanity in the face of suffering and about how to be a good person. Sure, kids come to school to learn English and maths and science and history and all the other subjects on the curriculum. But beyond all of that, and far more importantly, they come to school to learn how to be decent, well-rounded, kind, principled citizens. Looked at in that way, Liz's whole life was one long lesson.

I sit beside Zoe at the memorial service organised by the school. One student recalls being indifferent about French before ending up in Liz's A level group. He describes how she would allow them 'naughty days' when they could sit on the floor, eat sweets and read each other children's books in French. He says he didn't even realise he was learning and left school at eighteen a confirmed Francophile.

Amid the wave of tributes from students, former students, teachers, and her family, including her two remarkable teenage children who attend the school, Zoe and I agree that without Liz it's hard to see how we'd have made it this far in our careers without throwing in the towel or being sacked, or some combination of the two.

Mrs Thistletwat

I learned from Liz as much as anybody that there is a joy in taking kids out of the confines of bells and timetables and corridors and into the real world. Chicago confirmed for me that school trips are where you get the chance to know the students in a different environment, while opening their eyes to new experiences.

I run trips to West End theatres. Generally speaking, the kids are great, and a joy to spend the evening with, although I have perfected my patter threatening any child who so much as rustles a sweet paper during the show with detentions from now to Christmas.

On one occasion I've brought sixty Year 9s to watch a production of *Blood Brothers*. We're standing in an alleyway outside the theatre and some of the students are blocking the path of rush-hour commuters. After a couple of attempts to politely draw their attention to their unfortunate positioning I hear myself shout, 'Stand against the wall.' In fairness they do so immediately, but to my horror I notice that one unsuspecting member of the public has also followed my instruction, apparently thinking he was the victim of the world's least subtle mugging. I assure him that he is free to go about his business.

There's another theatre trip that will stay with me for a long time. Someone has recommended a show called *Avenue Q*. They told me it was a hilarious puppet show, brilliantly satirical and extremely witty. I suggest to another teacher that we take our Year 10s. She says she thinks a Shakespeare production at the Globe might be more appropriate, but I argue for the importance of contemporary drama and she reluctantly gives way. We send letters home with details and the trip quickly sells out.

In the period of time between selling all the tickets and the trip itself, I have a chance to go and see *Avenue Q* and my blood runs cold. It's full of swearing. One of the characters is called Mrs Thistletwat. There's a song called 'Everyone's A Little Bit Racist'. And worst of all there's an extended puppet sex scene, featuring several positions.

I get back to school and have no choice but to write to the parents of everyone who has signed up, warning that the content is a little more adult than I might have realised. None pull out of the trip, but when the day comes every swear word feels like a stab to the heart. As the puppets contort their naked furry bodies on stage, the teacher who favoured Shakespeare makes eye contact with me and gently shakes her head. Needless to say, the kids absolutely love it.

Working in Your Sleep

Julie the drama teacher is holding court in the staffroom about what happened to her last night. According to her husband, in the middle of the night she sat bolt upright and started moving kids into groups in her sleep. She was saying, 'You over here, let's have you in group 3 and Josie you're in group 6, please. And no back chat.' Then she lay down again and carried on sleeping as if nothing had happened. Pete, Julie's husband, said he was used to her teacher persona rearing its head from time to time in their waking life, but he drew the line at it infiltrating his sleep.

Coming Out to Kathy

In one of my line management meetings with Kathy, I tell her that I've recently started telling people I'm gay and she is typically affirming and supportive. But her next question takes me by surprise: 'Are you going to tell the kids?'

My first reaction is absolutely, categorically not. I'm there to teach them English, not confide in them. It feels like such a private, personal thing – why would I want to share it with a group of kids? Besides that, lots of parents would hate it – they'd see it as indoctrination and a breach of the boundary that should exist between teachers and pupils. There would definitely be complaints. I tell Kathy it hasn't even entered my head.

She listens patiently and says she understands my concerns, but she lays out the case for doing so. It obviously wouldn't be a big announcement; it would just be dropped into a wider discussion on something else. Good teachers tell stories all the time to illustrate points. If a maths teacher who is teaching ratios, say, can tell a story about going shopping with her husband and them arguing about what weight of flour they need in order to ensure they have enough to bake a cake for fifteen people instead of the six in the recipe, why shouldn't I tell an anecdote which mentions a boyfriend? Let's put to one side, for a moment, the fact that I don't have a boyfriend.

There might be the odd complaint, she says, but probably not many, and I would have her full support and that of the head in dealing with them. (Happily the head seems to have forgiven me for cupping his wife's breast.) My mentioning that I have a boyfriend in passing is unlikely to turn their son or daughter into a raving homosexual on the spot.

But more than that, she says, there will be kids sitting in my classes who are not straight. While many may be comfortable in their skins, others will be feeling isolated and lonely, and seeing someone in my position talking about being gay could be the boost they need. There will also, she says, be some kids who sit in front of me every day with deeply rooted homophobic attitudes inherited from their parents. They may not have worked closely with an openly gay person before. Given that I have a good working relationship with my classes, and that there is on the whole an atmosphere of mutual respect, my coming out could at least start the process of changing some of their minds.

They're all powerful arguments, but I'm ashamed to say that I don't do it. My fear of what might happen is just too great. In the last decade or so things have moved on enormously, and I hope that a young teacher finding themselves in that position today would feel confident to be themselves, including in the classroom.

Looking back I regret not being braver. But, to quote one of the most horrific, nauseating and patronising phrases teachers sometimes use: 'There's no such thing as FAIL. It actually stands for "First Attempt in Learning".' It's an appalling acronym. But it is true.

Mockingbird

I'm teaching *To Kill a Mockingbird* by Harper Lee to a bright, engaged, thoughtful Year 11 group and it's an unadulterated joy. I studied it when I was at school, and the lazy, slow-paced description of Scout's childhood games takes me back to those summer afternoons in Mrs Webb's classroom, being introduced to the pleasure that literature can bring. It's one of my favourite books; we named our cat Atticus after Atticus Finch, the great hero of the book.

The book's message of sticking up for the vulnerable and those who don't have a voice in society is as relevant today as it was when *To Kill a Mockingbird* was published back in 1960. For students at a school like ours, which is fairly ethnically homogeneous, this is essential reading.

An email comes in from the mother of one of the students in the class.

Dear Mr Wilson,

I am getting in touch about the book you have chosen to study with your Year 11 group, which includes my daughter. As a supportive parent I take a keen interest in the work she does and happened to be reading some of the text myself. I was shocked, not to mention appalled when I saw that the n- word occurs several times in this book. Please could you explain your rationale for choosing a novel with language of this sort to study with teenagers? Presumably, as a teacher, you should not be in the business of promoting racist language. Although we are white, I can't imagine what any black students must feel. I await your urgent response.

I read the letter several times, at a loss for how to respond. Having ranted about it to anyone in the staffroom who'll listen, I decide it's best to start with the obvious: that, of course, the word in question is extremely offensive. That it carries the weight of centuries of evil and oppression and has the power to truly wound, beyond either her or my full comprehension as white people.

Then I address the assumption that I am in some way in control of which books the exam boards decide should be set texts across the whole country. It's fair to say that these are decisions taken so far above my pay grade that they are in a different stratosphere.

In the next paragraph of my response I ask whether she is really saying that it's okay to divorce this one word from all the context in which it's written? Part of what the students are learning is how the frame of reference affects language. Taking things out of context is something I'm specifically teaching them not to do. On the few occasions the word is used, Harper Lee puts it in the mouths of racist characters – characters whose behaviour is repugnant, who are shown time and again to be ignorant, selfish and cruel. So far from 'promoting' racist language, it's showing it for what it is.

For goodness' sake, the whole point of the book is that we need to look out for those with less power in our society, which in 1930s Alabama most certainly included black people. It's one of the most famous anti-racist novels of all time. I find it staggering that anyone would suggest it promotes racism. I hope my response communicates some of my surprise without betraying quite how incredulous I am.

It reminds me of a similar incident from a few years previously. In the anthology of poems which students have to study for GCSE, there was one called 'Education for Leisure' by Carol Ann Duffy. It opens with the line, 'Today I am going to kill something. Anything.' The poem wonders about the mindset of a person who deliberately sets out to cause harm to someone else. At one point the speaker describes grabbing a breadknife and heading out on the streets.

When I taught it, it provoked really considered and nuanced discussions about the reasons people might get involved in criminality, from poverty to insecurity to boredom, to a feeling that they have little power or control in their lives, to the idea that some people might just be inherently evil. We would talk about the problem of knife crime, and what they would do to combat it if they were in charge. I would get them to practise their persuasive writing by drafting a letter to their MP saying what they would like him or her to do about it.

Unfortunately, an exam invigilator in a school somewhere complained that the poem was glorifying knife crime. They thought that a poem that is *clearly* anti-knife crime glorifies knife crime. The quote from this woman at the time was, 'I think it is absolutely horrendous – what sort of message is that to give to kids who are reading it as part of their GCSE syllabus?'

What sort of message? A message that knife crime is one of the ills of our society and we need to think very carefully about how we combat it.

You'd like to think that the exam board would have given the complaint short shrift but, inexplicably as far as I'm concerned, they withdrew the poem from the anthology with immediate effect. Not only that, but they asked schools to pulp any copies of the anthology they might have which featured the poem.

I'd like to ask that invigilator, 'What sort of a message does *that* send out?' That knife crime doesn't matter? That we shouldn't talk about important but difficult subjects? That censorship is to be encouraged? That all literature must only feature nice things and nothing controversial?

Carol Ann Duffy herself made the point in the aftermath of the ban that Shakespeare is rather heavy on the old knife crime too, so if we're banning 'Education for Leisure' we're also going to have to ban *Romeo and Juliet*, *Hamlet*, *Julius Caesar* ... And if we're going to wait for a novel in which no fictional character does anything remotely reprehensible or morally questionable, we might be waiting rather a long time. And wouldn't it be the most boring novel imaginable?

Duffy had the last laugh though; she wrote a poem addressed to the invigilator who complained, in which she blasted her arguments, and shortly afterwards she was appointed Poet Laureate.

Daily Mail Headlines

A teacher friend has recommended a board game that she bought on eBay and has adapted and used to great success with her classes to help with revision. Central to the game is a brightly coloured plastic device which acts as a kind of water pistol. You announce the topic you'd like to revise – let's say it's persuasive writing techniques – and then point the device at each member of the class in turn. It beeps with increasing urgency over ten seconds until you deactivate it when a correct answer is given. If no correct answer is given it squirts a jet of water at the unlucky loser.

I am excited to try it with my bottom-set English group. I think it'll add a bit of excitement and jeopardy to a potentially dull revision lesson. It starts off brilliantly.

'Tom, give me any example of an adjective.' Beep … beep … beep …

'Emmmmmmmm.'

'Come on, Tom, it's a describing word, remember?' Beepbeepbeep.

'Green?'

'Brilliant, Tom!' There's a round of applause and Tom stays dry.

'Joe, can you give us a verb?' Beep … beep … beep.

'Football?' Joe gets a jet of water to the face, I pass him a tissue to dry himself off, we all have a good laugh and then I spend a few minutes explaining why 'football' was a wrong answer.

The kiss of death: I allow myself to think this is going rather well.

We work our way around the room and next up is Lucy. Lucy is a sparky, engaged girl, full of life and spirit, who happens to have Down Syndrome. I hesitate a little. Is it fair to expect Lucy to play the game? In the couple of seconds I have to think about it, it occurs to me that the cardinal sin would be to leave Lucy out of the game. So I make the question as simple and straightforward as I can – something like, 'What's your favourite word?' – and delay as long as possible before starting the timer. But despite all the help that her learning support assistant and I try to give her, Lucy doesn't say a word.

There's another lightning decision to be made here. Do I go ahead and squirt water at her if she doesn't get a word within the time? My brain says yes, it would be discriminatory not to. So the time runs out and the game shoots some water at Lucy. To my horror, and in slow motion, Lucy falls backwards off her chair onto the floor. As I help her up, and check she's okay, in my mind's eye I can see the *Daily Mail* headlines: 'Monster Teacher Uses Water Cannon to Blast Down Syndrome Girl Off Her Chair in Schoolroom Attack'.

Lucy, luckily, is fine, and her teaching assistant tells me that in actual fact she loved the game and was probably deliberately not giving an answer because she wanted to be sprayed with water. But that was the last time we played the water game.

Sports Day

The sun always seems to beat down on Sports Day. If you've never been a teacher, you might think that it's a nice chance to get out of the classroom, get a bit of fresh air and maybe even top up your tan. If you've ever darkened the door of a school at any point in your career, you'll know that it's closer to a living purgatory. Wherever you look there are children throwing up or fainting or both. Healthy rivalries between form groups quickly boil over into running battles. Pretty much everybody could do with a courtesy spray of deodorant.

It's against this backdrop that Zoe asks if she can have a quick word with me. I try not to look too eager to leave behind the malodorous eleven-year-olds preparing for their 100-metre glory, and nod my thanks to the nearest colleague who agrees to watch them for a few minutes in my absence. My mind is running through what Zoe might want to talk about. Perhaps one of the kids she teaches has done something spectacularly hilarious. Or maybe she has a story about the bumbling manager we often discuss on journeys home.

The best place for confidential conversations is, like all other places in schools, unglamorous. It's a stationery cupboard. Surrounded by piles of textbooks and packets of pens, Zoe tells me that she has found a lump on her breast.

I say all the things you would say. It's good you're going to get it checked out. I'm sure it'll be nothing. People get lumps all the time. We hug. She's shaking.

Moving On

Somehow five years have slipped by since we qualified as teachers, and my time in the leafy suburbs is coming to an end. It's been a learning curve. It's been a colossal amount of work, not only in the school building but most evenings at home. It's been frustrating and triumphant and infuriating and brilliant. But overall it's been a blast, and I'll miss it tremendously.

The allure of London, however, has proved too great. Of course I'm sad to leave Zoe, not least because of what she's just told me, but I'm not moving too far away. In the last year since coming out, it's felt like a logical next step to broaden my horizons and give city life a go, so I've taken up a job as head of English at a school that could scarcely be more different from the one I'm leaving. It's an inner-city comprehensive in a very deprived area. More than 90 per cent of the kids are from an ethnic minority background, many have little or no English, and it seems as though every other child has a back story that would melt even the hardest of hearts. It's going to be a challenge.

Management

The mildly terrifying prospect I face is leading a team of eighteen English teachers. And the first item on the agenda for September is a departmental meeting that I am to chair. The night before has been torrid and sleepless as I run over in my head all the things that could go wrong at that meeting. What if someone disagrees fundamentally with what I say about education? What if I accidentally go momentarily mad and say insulting things? What if there is an out-and-out rebellion and everyone just refuses to work?

In the event, my new colleagues are enthusiastic, committed and willing to welcome me into their midst. The only controversy is that some teachers feel there aren't enough Pritt sticks to go around their classes. One teacher sends an email around the department accusing other teachers of taking more Pritt sticks than they were entitled to from the stationery cupboard. By the time I get back to my office from a meeting there are a dozen emails about glue, with claims and counter-claims of who was responsible for the drought. I should have foreseen it; glue is like gold bullion in schools. I take a deep breath, send an email saying I will order another two hundred glue sticks for immediate delivery, and reflect on how you can never predict where the issues are going to arise.

Mind Your Language

The head teacher of my new school is Paul. He's a warm guy in his fifties, who every now and then shows flashes of a steely core that reminds you that you wouldn't want to get on his bad side. He is supportive of his new head of English and always has time for a chat in the corridor. 'I'll pop in and see one of your lessons some time if you don't mind,' he says. The only real response to that is, 'Of course, that would be brilliant,' so that is what I say. The days go past, then a few weeks, and I assume that maybe he didn't mean that he would actually come and observe the lesson. Maybe he was just showing polite interest and the visit was hypothetical.

I am teaching my lively Year 10s one Wednesday morning. The topic is the formality of language, and how we adapt the register we use to suit specific circumstances. To get them thinking along the right lines, I have projected a photo of Paul onto the whiteboard as they come into the classroom. I've added a speech bubble to the photo; he is saying, 'Good morning, how are you today?' My bright idea is that we will brainstorm various responses to that question, arrange them in order of formality, and then discuss which would be appropriate when speaking to the head teacher.

I open my mouth to begin the lesson and am aware in my peripheral vision of some movement outside the classroom. To my absolute horror, I see Paul walking towards the door and coming in. 'Good morning, Mr Wilson, do you mind if I join you for this lesson?' he asks. 'Of course not,' I lie, and I have a full-body cringe as he takes a seat at the back of the room and spots his own face smiling back at him from the whiteboard.

I proceed to ask the class how they would respond to that greeting from the head teacher. The kids show zero embarrassment or restraint despite the fact that the man in question is mere feet away from them. 'All right, sir!' is about the most repeatable of the responses. 'Suck my dick, sir,' is one of the less ideal ripostes.

As an aside, being called 'sir' or 'miss' is one of the bizarre aspects of teaching, and I never quite get used to it. Some of my female colleagues used to argue, I think rightly, that 'miss' is less respectful than 'sir', and so some schools moved to 'madam' which might just be differently bad. But in any case the titles have become so ubiquitous that they no longer communicate much sense of respect: it's not uncommon to hear a child say, 'Fuck off, sir.'

I brazen my way through the rest of my planned exercise and try to calmly underline types of register. As Paul leaves the room with a 'thank you' and a hint of a smile, my blood pressure takes the rest of the day to return to normal.

Test Results

Zoe's lump is breast cancer. It's unfair and outrageous and crushing. She is stoic and philosophical but sad. She faces her chemotherapy with characteristic grit. Like Liz, she continues working, throwing herself into her teaching with her usual enthusiasm and energy.

Amongst the horror and the tears and the worry there is lovely news. Zoe has started dating Dan (of door-handle fame) from the department, and he is already providing the emotional support she needs. It's strange but wonderful to see my two friends together, and it's clear right from the start that Dan will help her get through the tough months ahead.

Zoe too has had a promotion. She's a head of year, responsible for the academic progress and pastoral care of a whole year group. I am not there to witness it, but everyone agrees that she is a natural. She has exactly the right balance of nurturing empathy and no-nonsense common sense. If Zoe can take responsibility for three hundred kids and make it look easy, surely cancer doesn't stand a chance.

Results are King

Plenty of jobs are high pressure. Doctors are required to make life or death decisions every day. If you're a builder it must be pretty stressful making sure your structure will withstand a storm. And if you're working on a checkout on a busy Saturday afternoon you have the unrelenting queue to keep down. The challenge of being a teacher, and particularly of being the head of a core department, comes from the fact that no matter what you do, or how hard you work, your success in your role is largely judged on the achievements of teenagers. And teenagers, in case you weren't aware, rarely top lists of the most reliable people.

At around the time I took up the post as head of English, the ante was being upped. The spotlight was on results like never before. Some incentive for teachers to push students to achieve their best is, of course, healthy. But this single-minded obsession with grades was the opposite of healthy.

There are a number of people to blame for the toxic atmosphere which was bubbling up in schools at that time, not least the then Education Secretary Michael Gove. But let's start with the other Michael: Sir Michael Wilshaw.

Wilshaw was Ofsted's chief inspector for five long years from 2012 until 2016. On paper he was great. He'd been head of Mossbourne Academy in Hackney, where there's no doubt he did a lot of good. He made it one of the best schools in the country. Friends of mine who worked there talked of a man who commanded respect, was tough, uncompromising and dogged in his pursuit of excellence for his students.

Great qualities for someone charged with the overseeing of British schools, you might think. And it's true that much of his rhetoric was impressive, even inspiring. Standards and progress were his watchwords. Only through a relentless focus on raising standards could we truly improve the life chances of the most deprived pupils, the spiel went. No arguments there from me. So what went wrong?

Well, firstly he rubbed staff up the wrong way. He criticised a culture of teachers heading 'out the gate at three o'clock', though all the teachers I knew were at work until much later and then took marking and lesson plans home for evenings and weekends. He said it was teachers' responsibility to stand up to and even fine bad parents, which put staff at risk, threatened vital relationships and further distracted teachers from their core work. And most offensively of all, as schools struggled to recruit teachers and others left due to unmanageable workloads, he claimed, 'If anyone says to you that "staff morale is at an all-time low" you know you are doing something right.'

Everyone wants to feel valued and appreciated in their work. Those kind of undermining comments make it even more challenging to face Year 9 on a wet Wednesday afternoon. But ultimately teachers are a pretty resilient bunch, and if he had been doing otherwise brilliant work, I reckon most of us would have bitten our lips and secretly admired him.

The real issue is that his understandable, even admirable, focus on exam results and pupil achievement became an obsession. This had already been the direction of travel prior to Wilshaw, but he accelerated it. Ofsted put more and more and more emphasis on stats. Exam results data gained a stranglehold on schools. The feeling was, with plenty of justification, that even before an Ofsted inspector crossed the threshold of your school they would have made their judgement, because they would have internalised every aspect of the school's exam data.

I suppose it's the thing about schools that is easiest to measure; the numbers are there in black and white. But it ignores so much work that is not easily measurable; the happiness of students, their extracurricular involvement, the extent to which they are taught to be responsible citizens or how well they look after each other.

And that data Ofsted obsesses over contains more information than just how many kids pass their exams. It indicates whether boys and girls are achieving equally. Whether there's any ethnic group that's lagging behind. Whether children on free school meals are doing as well as those who aren't. Whether departments are equal in terms of achievement. Whether all pupils have made enough progress from primary school. Whether targets have been met in each and every one of those areas.

Teachers should, and in my experience do, consider these things as part of their work. It is essential that we help all pupils achieve their best, whatever their gender, race or background, and the stats can be useful signposts to help focus minds on underachieving groups. But when so much emphasis is put on data alone, and the stakes are so high – a damning Ofsted report can easily end a head teacher's career – our real priorities can be lost. Heads become understandably stressed and overburdened with the frankly impossible task of making sure all those numbers stay where they're supposed to be. Leadership teams, which should be thinking about how they can better meet the needs of all the families they serve, how they can improve the school community, how they can engage more kids in learning, end up spending all their time colour-coding spreadsheets.

Head teachers are not at the chalkface, so they pass their own stress on to heads of department who in turn are encouraged to crunch data rather than focus on what's going on with their teams. They inevitably communicate that anxiety to classroom teachers who transfer it to students. You end up with a school community operating on a knife edge, where you can feel the panic barely concealed beneath the hubbub in every corridor.

And kids aren't robots. No matter how good the teaching they've received, no matter how many revision sessions they've been to, no matter how many spreadsheets have been analysed, their performance is unpredictable. A drop in any one of those numbers in any given year isn't necessarily a cause for concern. It's the nature of the beast.

And even if all the numbers are brilliant, what does that mean? We've succeeded in teaching kids to pass exams.

Great. Is that really our ultimate aim for our education system? Kids have learned exam technique. The school is branded outstanding by Ofsted. Hurrah.

I'd much rather children attend schools which look at their exam results, but don't obsess over them. Which value teachers who inspire and care and are passionate, not just those who churn out results. I'd like them to study in an environment where they don't feel they're under the cosh at all times. And I'd like schools to value education in its broadest sense, preparing children for exams but also, more importantly, preparing them for life after they walk out the school gates for the last time.

I was fortunate to work under head teachers who were level-headed and sensible and did their best to shield their staff from the very worst of the pressure. But they weren't able to provide complete insulation, and they shouldn't have to.

There were times as head of department when I felt I was swimming against the tide, whilst getting pelted with missiles by the Department for Education and Ofsted. I was constantly trying to do what was best for the children we taught, whilst having to pay lip service to all manner of initiatives born out of the belief that every child must have their progress in every subject monitored at every moment.

Like a nightmare version of the Chuckle Brothers, the two Michaels, Gove and Wilshaw, wrought untold damage on the education system of this country. Both of their reigns were terrible for schools, but in a way Wilshaw was worse, partly because he was in post longer, and also because as a teacher himself he should have known better.

During his time as chief inspector, Ofsted damaged the schools it was responsible for improving. Its limited conception of successful teaching and obsession with data is a large part of the reason teachers rightly complain about stress and workload and why so many decided to leave a profession which at times felt as though the fun and the joy had been drained out of it. I hope the organisation and its leaders have grown to value the breadth and complexity of this vocation, and there are some signs that things have improved in the years since. But progress, as Ofsted would put it, is not fast enough.

What's Wrong with You?

One of many things to get used to in the new role is that teachers will now send unruly children to me. This is a good thing, as it means their lessons proceed without needless interruptions, and the remaining children can get on with learning. The only teeny downside is that it presumes I will know how to deal with them.

An occasion when that is resolutely not the case is with Alicia, a Year 10 student who has been sent out of her GCSE English lesson. In my experience boys tend to act up much more often than girls, but it's more difficult to defuse confrontational situations with girls. When boys are challenged on their behaviour they will often flare up, perhaps even become aggressive, but next lesson they'll walk in and say, 'All right, sir,' and all is forgotten. Girls will sometimes hold it against you until the day they leave the school. These are stereotypes, of course, but there's definitely some truth to them.

I arrive at the classroom in question to find Alicia teetering outside the door on shoes that add inches to her height and with a little bag dangling from her elbow. I encourage her to come with me to my office. I try to balance authority and compassion in my voice as I say, 'OK, Alicia, probably best if you come with me please.' I am ill-prepared for the ferocity of the response.

'What? Why would I want to come with *you*? I'm going to stay here. There is nothing you can do to move me. What's wrong with you?'

My response is comparatively meek. 'Come on, Alicia. There's an easy way and a hard way to do this. Let's just go and sit down and talk about whatever has happ—' I don't finish my sentence because she has held up her hand to stop me speaking. She is looking at a female teacher who happens to be walking along the corridor towards her.

'OMG, miss! I love your shoes. Where did you get them?' She looks back at me: 'You can continue with whatever you were saying in a minute.'

I am so shocked that I don't really know what to say. I don't have a clue what to do and it's a terrible feeling. Clearly her behaviour is appalling, and she has no intention of doing anything I say. But I'm meant to be here to sort the situation out! I have a walkie-talkie and could radio for support from other colleagues; it just feels like such a failure to admit that I don't really know what to do with a fifteen-year-old girl. After a bit more arguing I conclude that I have no choice. A deputy head arrives and Alicia immediately agrees to go with her.

'I'm so glad you're here, miss. I definitely wouldn't go with that other guy. He was so rude to me,' she says, making sure it's loud enough for me to hear.

I feel suddenly lonely. There's not even anyone to talk to about this whole unsettling experience. I can't really share it with other teachers in the department as I'm supposed to be supporting them, and I'm reluctant to go to senior colleagues as they are all busy with their own issues and I worry it would make me look weak. I can't even discuss it with Zoe on the way home.

Come On

The art of being a head of department, I'm discovering, is learning to cope with the guilt. There are so many demands on your time, so much admin, so many people you need to talk to on a daily basis, so much data analysis, that often your lessons, by far the most important part of your work, can take something of a back seat. At my school full-time teachers teach twenty-one hour-long lessons every week, and as head of department I teach eighteen, so there is still a lot of planning and marking to be done alongside everything else.

The kids here behave quite differently from those I taught in Essex. They are generally more streetwise, tougher, more likely to argue back. Every discussion is spirited, they wear their hearts on their sleeves, and they are not shy about telling you what they think. If they are finding a lesson dull they'll certainly let you know, but equally when they have enjoyed it they'll thank you with sincerity beyond anything I experienced in the suburbs. And, ultimately, kids are kids, wherever in the world you happen to encounter them.

From the start I have had a real soft spot for my Year 10 class. They're sparky and chatty and patient with a teacher who is clearly out of his depth when pronouncing their names. One particular morning I write the word 'Homework' on the board, and begin jotting down the activities they will need to complete for the next lesson. There is a predictable groan from the class.

'Awww, sir, come on,' one student begs.

I turn to look at them. 'Year 10,' I begin, 'please do not "Come on" me.'

A pause as the horror of what I have just said sinks in. One child lets out a nasal snigger at the back of the room. Then I am trying with every fibre of my being not to laugh. And before I know it the class have erupted, and I'm pretending I have no idea what they're laughing at.

Mobile Phones

The top three things that will ruin any lesson:

Coming in at number one, it's a wasp in the classroom. Not a single person will be listening to a word you say, and there will be a Mexican-wave effect of kids standing up and flapping their arms completely ineffectually as the creature tours the room. You might as well give up and go home.

A close second is snow. The white stuff appears and any class, from the young ones up to the oldest, are instantly transfixed. It ranks below wasps because at least they are quietly and calmly not listening as opposed to loudly and overexcitedly.

But a message tone or – even more so – a ringing mobile phone isn't far behind wasps and snow for ruining your carefully crafted lesson. All heads in the room, the teacher's included, will swivel, looking for the source of the sound. One child will glow a brilliant shade of red and guiltily grab their vibrating pocket. And everyone will hold their breath, waiting to see what happens next.

Mobiles are banned completely in both schools I have worked at. If they're seen at all, we're supposed to confiscate them, put them in an envelope and deliver them to the relevant head of year, from whom the student can collect the phone if they bring along a note from their parent confirming that they can have it back. That might sound a little draconian. Over the years there has been a bit of a pro-phone movement from some parents' groups. I imagine it's the same ones who think that putting their child in a nice classroom away from their friends when they have beaten someone up is against their human rights.

They generally say that their child needs a mobile phone so that they can get a message to them in case of an emergency. Well, you can do that via the school reception, so let's discount that. The other argument, and one that I have some sympathy for, is that it's useful to have in case they get into difficulty on their way to or from school. Leaving aside the fact that quite a lot of the parents who make this argument are the same ones who drive their kids to the school gates and pick them up there at the end of the day, I can see that as a parent that could give you some peace of mind.

But you have to compare that advantage with the problems caused by giving children so much access to the internet with so little supervision. We have certificates for films, and we police who we think they're suitable for, but it seems many parents are happy to give their child a device which allows them to access everything and anything online, at an age when they aren't necessarily able to process what's right and what's wrong, what's real and what's fake, what's normal and what's extreme. Of course, this is an argument against kids having phones generally but teachers, who are acting in loco parentis, are simply not able to monitor what children are accessing online if they have their phones in school.

There has been much reporting about how social media sites exacerbate problems with body image, self-esteem and eating disorders. But the cases of bullying by messaging services that I've witnessed are also truly shocking. Whereas in days gone by a victim could often retreat to the relative safety of their bedroom at the end of the day and get some respite, for as long as they are carrying a mobile they are accessible to the bullies at all times.

I've seen pupils form Facebook groups where their entire *raison d'être* is to post insults and unflattering photos of a particular person. I've seen WhatsApp groups which are set up solely to be nasty about another child; they will sometimes briefly invite the child in question to join the group, just for long enough that they know the discussion is happening, and then kick them out again. And sometimes the victim is FaceTimed by a group of the perpetrators who proceed to carry out remote bullying. Of course you can say they should block the numbers or simply not answer, but bullies often show remarkable ingenuity in getting around such barriers.

Sexting is also a massive problem. A young, insecure girl or boy is approached by a predatory child, maybe an older pupil, and showered with praise about their appearance. Maybe they're even asked out on a date. They're so flattered that, perhaps against their better judgement, they allow themselves to be persuaded to send a naked picture to the other child. Within an hour that photo has done the rounds on countless messaging services, most kids in the school have seen it, and the original child is mortified, filled with shame, and doesn't want to come to school any more – and they can't even tell their parents what's wrong. It's a pattern I've seen play out more times than I can remember.

Against this backdrop the other problems with mobile phones seem relatively minor. They ring or buzz in class and disrupt the lesson. They are inevitably stolen from PE changing rooms or lockers, and the ensuing investigations take up enormous swathes of staff time while rarely recovering the phone. And all this doesn't even touch on the wider issue of the damage done to traditional face-to-face communication by people who walk around with their eyes locked on a screen the whole time. Occasionally I see groups of three or four students sitting on the playing field at lunch, not talking to each other for their entire break while they tap away illicitly at their phones, and it strikes me as rather sad.

Forgive the rant; if it's any consolation, this is an abridged version of what any child I caught on their phone received.

That's Assault

One of the first big set-piece events of the academic year is the Year 11 mock exam. Nearly two hundred and fifty sixteen-year-olds together in the school hall sitting a two-hour paper which will be marked by their teachers, in order to give them an insight into their strengths and weaknesses before they have to do the real thing. It's my job to get the exam started, reminding the kids of the rules, and to end it, telling them when time is up and they need to hand in their papers.

The other teachers in the department are standing around the edge of the hall, and I know that I am speaking not only to the children, but to them. They're watching to see how I cope in this role, how I interact with the children and whether this young guy who taught at a nice school in the suburbs can cope at a London comp.

'Put your pens down,' I say as the time is up, 'and wait to be dismissed by staff row by row. You are still under exam conditions until you're out of the room so that means absolutely no talking, please.' It's a pretty standard spiel.

We're letting the kids go when one boy right in front of me starts chatting loudly to two friends as he walks out of the hall. 'Excuse me,' I say, 'no talking, please.' He definitely hears me because he's only a couple of feet away, but he ignores me. I try again. 'Excuse me. I'm talking to you. Could you be quiet, please?' Again nothing. On my third attempt he turns around, looks me in the eye and says under his breath, but very distinctly, 'Fuck off.' I am stunned.

He walks around the corner. At this point I make a critical error, borne of the hubristic need not to appear weak in front of my colleagues. I pick up my pace and turn the corner after him. The golden rule is, *Never follow them!* Later, when they and you have both calmed down, go and find them and talk it out. That way you have the hope of maintaining some dignity. But that ship has sailed this time.

I'm behind him again and I am saying, 'Excuse me,' on repeat like some sort of demented serial sneezer. He ignores me. I reach out and put my hand on his shoulder from behind and say, 'Can we have a chat, please?' I rest my hand on his shoulder without applying any pressure at all. I don't stop him, I don't turn him around, and I certainly don't hit him. But he is quick as a flash. 'Arrggghhhh.' It's the kind of noise you would expect a human to make if you had just punched them in the stomach whilst pulling out all their hair and telling them that their family had sadly died: it's a primal, guttural, scream.

'That is ASSAULT,' he says no less loudly. By now people are stopping in the corridor to watch what's going on. 'This guy has just assaulted me,' he says, gesticulating at me to other students and any of my new colleagues who happen to be passing. I cannot believe that anyone would even attempt to call what I did assault. It's like when footballers fall theatrically to the ground when another player brushes past them.

I explain to him, calmly, that I want to have a chat about what exam conditions mean, and about him telling me to eff off only a couple of minutes earlier. 'I'm going to report that assault,' he threatens. I tell him, not entirely truthfully, that I don't mind what he does; it doesn't change the fact that we need to talk about his behaviour.

Our conversation is fairly one-sided because it consists of me restating the obvious: that you shouldn't tell your teacher to fuck off. I send him on his way and don't think much more of it until days later when Paul, the head teacher, turns up at the door of my office to tell me that he's had a report that a Year 11 has gone off his food and hasn't slept since he was assaulted by me.

I can feel my blood cooling in my veins. An allegation of violence can easily spell the end of a career whether it is proven or not. I assume that I will be suspended with immediate effect, something schools can do 'as a neutral act' while investigations take place.

The effect such suspensions have on the member of staff concerned is, of course, anything but neutral. When someone disappears overnight and nothing is said about what's happened to them, the staffroom rumour mill goes into overdrive. The worst bit is that the individual is bound by confidentiality clauses which mean they can't even defend themselves. And if teachers are gossiping, the kids are too, not to mention their parents. That's what's going through my head as Paul stands in the doorway telling me that he has set up a meeting to talk through the allegations that afternoon.

Fortunately for me, Paul is a reasonable man. He tells me that the kid has made unfounded allegations before and reassures me that, having spoken to others who were around at the time, he believes my version of events. Later, after the meeting, he tells me that he's not going to suspend me. As I reflect on the day's events I feel sorry for the child that his natural response to any sort of accusation is to lash out and that he sees violence in any contact. It must be exhausting to be always fighting like that.

A few weeks later I end up taking over his class and teaching him the end of his GCSE course. I see a softer, more vulnerable side to him. His mother died when he was very young and in his short life he has already experienced violence. It takes my mind back to Martha and the threats she made at the primary school several years previously. Two very different students in two very different circumstances, but similar troubled backgrounds and a similar ability to strike the fear of God into me. I can't stop thinking about how that one misguided touch on the shoulder could have brought my whole career crashing down.

Carol Ann Duffy

My other Year 10 class is the so-called 'bottom set' although it's not a term I like. In fact, I'm not mad keen on setting by ability full stop. The danger is that sets give the impression that ability is static, and can become a self-fulfilling prophecy, with the higher sets receiving a confidence boost which helps them perform well, and the lower sets receiving a message that they're not expected to succeed. Some schools try to get around this by naming the classes after famous authors, so you might have Dickens class and Rowling class rather than set 3 or set 7, but I think all kids are bright enough to work out where they have been put in the pecking order.

The problem is that I can't think of a better model. In principle, I like the idea of mixed-ability teaching. Students who aren't performing so well can watch those who are and learn from them, while those who are achieving the higher grades realise just how fortunate they are to be doing so. And after all, life – society – is mixed ability.

But in my experience it comes under the category of 'good in principle but a nightmare in practice'. When you have thirty-two children in a class, with target grades ranging from A* to F, the complexity of making sure that the high fliers are being stretched and those who struggle most are being supported, and everyone in between is also being pushed, is just too great. And you might be trying to do that five times a day.

The compromise I introduce in my department is to have a big top set where kids can be really pushed towards the highest grades, several middle sets which are fairly mixed ability, and a small class of those who need lots of one-to-one input. We aim to encourage teachers to move children between classes where appropriate so they don't get stuck in a class which isn't challenging them.

As head of department there is a tacit understanding that you'll take the trickier classes, which are often the lower sets. Their behaviour can be erratic, they're often disengaged, they bring that baggage I described earlier from years of thinking and being told that they 'aren't academic' or 'can't do English'. But there is a pleasure in the challenge of trying to turn it around for them. Naturally it isn't always possible. You fail more than you succeed. Sometimes it feels as though you never win. But when you do the sense of achievement and celebration for that child is unparalleled.

There is a young man in this class called Azad. Where some of the others are lethargic he is sparky and engaged. He struggles with comprehension and he finds writing difficult, but he has bags of personality, and I really like him. I've been teaching the work of the Poet Laureate, Carol Ann Duffy, who has by now hopefully recovered from the ignominy of having her poem about knife crime wiped from the exam board anthology. On this particular day we're looking at one of her love poems.

'Who is the bloke she's writing them to?' Azad shouts out.

Calmly and quietly I ask him why he's so sure that she was writing to a bloke. 'As it happens, Azad, Carol Ann Duffy is in a relationship with a woman.'

Azad's mouth could scarcely have opened wider had it been wedged with a ruler. There is a bit of other tittering and nudging, but I try my best to make sure that this news is delivered in as low-key a way as possible.

A year later Azad comes bounding up to me in the corridor.

'Sir, sir,' he says, 'I saw that fat lesbian you taught us about died.'

I have to pause for a moment and try to piece together what on earth is going on inside his head. After a few seconds of confused silence I ask him, 'Are you talking about Margaret Thatcher, Azad?' She had died the day before and I can't imagine who else he might mean.

'Yeah, the gay poet.'

Taking a deep breath, I explain that the poet was actually Carol Ann Duffy, not Margaret Thatcher, that Thatcher had been the first female prime minister of the UK but was not, so far as we know, a lesbian nor had she written poetry. I can see the cogs going around.

'Ah, I get it now,' he says, a smile breaking out across his face. 'Thanks, sir, for explaining.'

I begin walking down the corridor again, content that I have done a good deed in clarifying the significance of yesterday's death in young Azad's mind. I have taken a step and a half when my sense of satisfaction is interrupted by his voice.

'So Margaret Thatcher was dating Carol Ann Duffy who died?'

I have no idea how Thatcher and Duffy have become entwined in his head, but it's another reminder to never, ever feel pleased with yourself in teaching.

Champagne

Zoe comes to visit London now and again. We go for long walks and talk about our early days in teaching, wondering what some of those hilarious students we taught are up to now. We talk about her treatment, and how it is progressing well, and our hopes and plans for the future. Losing her hair has been particularly hard. I remember how she used to make me drive her right to the front door of the school if the wind was anything more than a gentle whisper, for fear that her do might be ruined. But she has an array of wigs, and she wears them really well.

Together, we remember the day we drove to Norwich by accident, the night Zoe misspelt 'respect' in a bar and the time she fell flat on her face in the corridor. And we remember Liz, whose illness has a new poignancy given Zoe's own. But her relationship with Dan is flourishing and, though there is an underlying sadness about her condition, she is happy.

On one occasion I say that I will take her for lunch. As I'm wondering where we should go, I'm struck anew by how this illness shows no regard for who it strikes or when, by how finely balanced and fragile our health and happiness are. In that spirit, I make a spur-of-the-moment decision to surprise her by taking her to one of the nicest restaurants in London. I tell her that she should dress up, and ignore her quip about how she never thought she'd see the day when I offered her advice about what to wear.

When the waiter asks whether we'd like anything to drink I hear myself say, 'Yes, we'll have some champagne, please,' as if I'm a City banker rather than a state school teacher. We have the most lovely afternoon, spending that time together. It is beyond a price.

That's Gay

Aside from being thrown by Margaret Thatcher's hitherto undiscovered gay trysts, I have come to terms a little more with my own sexuality. One thing that has helped is realising that, on the whole, things that seem like a massive deal in my head, are mostly of only passing interest to anybody else. Not in a nasty or uncaring way; it's just that everyone is fighting their own battles. There was one unfortunate moment when a well-meaning friend said, 'Well, of course, you'll never be able to get a job in a boys' school now,' but on the whole people are kind and supportive.

Thanks to *Guardian Soulmates*, and following some of the most awkward flirting that has ever occurred between two humans, I have acquired a boyfriend. All my new colleagues are aware of my orientation and while I didn't choose to mention anything about a partner in front of the kids, I have brought him along to a couple of school functions.

I am covering a lesson for a colleague, and explain to the class that their teacher is away but has left them some work to get on with. 'Man, that is gay,' says a boy in the front row. I don't react, but continue to explain the tasks that are to keep them occupied.

As I sit at my desk while they get on with their work, though, I can't stop thinking about the boy's comment that it's 'gay' that they have to do some cover work. It's not uncommon, of course. Kids say that their homework, or their detention, or their pencil cases are gay all the time. But this time, perhaps because I am more at ease with myself, I feel confident enough to say something.

I ask the boy if we can have a chat outside. He's genuinely confused about what he's done wrong. He's by no means a bad kid. But I explain to him that he used 'gay' interchangeably with 'annoying' or 'stupid' and that could be seen as offensive.

'Yeah, but there aren't any gay people in there, sir.'

Choosing my words carefully, I explain that he doesn't know that, and he can't know who might be wrestling in silence with their sexual orientation. However innocent his intentions, it's conceivable that the flippant use of the word 'gay' could make it more difficult for anyone in that position.

'Nah, sir,' he says. 'I know everyone in that room and none of them is gay. Trust me.'

I repeat that he can't be sure of that, and try to raise an eyebrow pointedly as I say, 'You just never know who you might be talking to who is actually gay.'

My attempts at subtlety fail and I decide I'll try again later. I find the whole episode a little demoralising; but, as it turns out, the teaching gods have ordained a scenario later that week which will restore equilibrium.

It's my bottom-set Year 10s, and they are working on presentations which they'll deliver to the class on a subject they feel passionate about. They can give their talk on anything they like, providing it's a topic they're genuinely interested in. They have a week to plan and rehearse, and before we know it the first day of presentations is upon us.

We endure half a dozen that don't deviate in their subject matter from football teams I've never heard of, motorbikes and various games consoles and their respective games. After each speaker has finished, they take questions from the class and I try to feign interest by asking something without betraying the fact that I have neither knowledge of, nor interest in, West Bromwich Albion.

Next up to give her presentation is a quiet girl called Zofia. Right from the outset I've been a bit worried about how she'll cope with public speaking. She hardly ever contributes when we have discussions in class, and too often she gets lost amongst some of the bigger characters. She moved to the UK from Poland several years ago and still has the accent. I have always felt that she hugely lacks confidence.

As she walks between the rows of desks to the front of the classroom I am mentally preparing how I will bail her out if she completely freezes. 'Not to worry,' I'll say. 'You gave it a really good shot. And it can be hard to speak in front of your peers. How about you and I give it another go some break time?'

But she has started speaking and is lucid, controlled and confident. She says that she is going to speak about LGBT+ rights in her home country. She talks about how distressing it is that people there aren't able to live their lives being true to themselves or expressing who they really are. She contrasts it with how accepting and tolerant London is. She's doing so well. The time comes for questions and one of the boys asks her why she chose that topic. She says that she's never really talked about it in school before, but that she is gay herself.

What happens next is mind-blowingly beautiful in the most low-key way. There is no cheering. No one hugs her or slaps her on the back or congratulates her. Instead this class of north London teenagers react to her presentation with the same lack of interest they have shown to the others. They clap politely and then they ask how long is left until lunchtime and whether we can watch a film next lesson. The revelation could not have caused less of a ripple. In fact, mine is the only brain in the room which is racing at what I have witnessed. I am overwhelmed with pride and pleasure at her bravery in being herself.

As the kids filter out of the classroom, I catch Zofia and tell her I am so impressed at her courage and her composure. She is instantly shy again. She says thanks and is gone.

I don't tell her that I'm also thinking of my sixteen-year-old self, and just how far we, as a society, have advanced. If someone had come out at my school I can't imagine what hellish existence they would have endured. During my whole time there no one did, to my knowledge, which speaks for itself. More than that, due in part I suppose to Section 28, which banned local authorities from 'promoting' homosexuality between 1988 and 2003, it was never even mentioned. Any reference to homosexuality was airbrushed from the study of history, English literature, drama, the arts and even health education. So the only time the word 'gay' was ever spoken in schools was as an insult in the playground. It's hard to over-estimate just how much psychological damage that may have done to a whole generation of young LGBT+ people.

As Zofia gave her speech, she couldn't have known the cocktail of emotions she was stirring in me. The contrast between the quiet confidence she exhibited, and the panicked fear I felt nearly twenty years previously was moving and fantastic. Zofia, and the entirely accepting nature of the rest of the class, are the reason that I am leaving school with a smile on my face today.

Dowry

Six years of teaching in English schools has significantly eroded my Northern Irish accent. It's a matter of necessity. This is a profession with communication at its heart, and if you can't make yourself easily understood, you aren't going to be doing a great job.

I was burned early on when trying to reprimand a girl who had skipped a lesson. As I ranted on about how disappointing it was because she had abused my trust blah blah blah she looked increasingly confused. Eventually she could take no more and said, 'Honestly, I can't understand a word you're saying. Are you African?'

Today I am teaching a poem that uses the word 'dowry'. I explain as clearly as I can what a dowry is, and move on to analyse the poem with the class. A couple of minutes later a hand goes up.

'Sir,' a girl sitting near the front says, 'I don't understand what a "dowry" actually is.'

Except that she pronounces the word in a perfect Northern Irish accent: something like 'doy-ree'. And now I not only have to explain what the word means again, I have to try to pronounce it like an English person.

2012 Results

While most people only have to go through the stress of collecting GCSE results once in their lifetime, for teachers it is an annual horror. By 2012, it was far from my first time at the rodeo and I had been lulled into a false sense of security because every time it had all turned out well. The kids I had taught had more or less got what they deserved, and quite often exceeded their and my expectations. Consequently results day, once the envelopes were opened, was almost entirely pleasant. It passed in a blur of excited screeches and congratulatory handshakes and general merriment. Of course some students were disappointed, but there was nearly always a reason why they had underperformed, and I don't recall any total calamities.

2012 is different though. For a start I am no longer just a classroom teacher. I am leading a team of eighteen teachers and have responsibility for the results of the whole department rather than just my own group. More than that, it is my first year in post so everyone from Paul down will be judging me based on these results. And while all grades matter to a school, those in English are especially important. The main figure on which a school is judged is the percentage of students who achieve five or more A*-C GCSE grades including English and maths. I can feel the sword of Damocles swinging perilously close to my head.

Results are actually released to schools on the day before the official results day. So that's why I find myself sitting in front of a computer at midnight downloading spreadsheet after spreadsheet of results data like a loser.

On some level I expect to experience that familiar feeling where things are much better than I had anticipated and I'm left wondering what the point was of all the worrying. But the more I look at the data, the clearer it is that something is wrong. All the kids we feared might get Ds have got Ds or Es – there is not even one who has bucked the trend. But much worse is that most of the kids we were pretty certain would get the magic C grade have come out with Ds too. Getting a C in English is your ticket to sixth form or college or getting a decent job. It's the grade that counts as a pass on the school stats. And time and time again the young people that we knew should get Cs have not done so.

I feel physically sick. I check the data and check it again to make sure I'm not making some kind of stupid mistake, and maybe everything is all right after all. But the more I check the worse it looks.

I head into school on the official results morning with all the enthusiasm of a sloth on Valium. I know that I will have to endure difficult conversations with the head about why these results look so different to our optimistic predictions. I know that for the next year at least senior management will be crawling all over our department in an effort to ensure that this doesn't happen again.

But most of all it's the kids. It's seeing them arrive and open the envelopes, hoping for the best but getting the worst. And it's trying to explain what's gone on to a group of dedicated and talented teachers who have slogged and encouraged and cajoled and commiserated with these kids over a period of several years. It's all just grim.

I decide that the only thing I can do, as I make the long journey to school that morning, is hope for some sort of miracle. It's not the most practical of strategies, granted, but in the absence of any other plan, miracles it is. And sure enough, a miracle comes.

I pass a newsagent's and catch a glimpse of a newspaper headline which mentions 'fury over GCSE English results'. The idea that it might not just be us – that it might not be our team, our department, me – to blame is a ray of light. Every word of the article I read makes me feel incrementally less terrible and more angry.

The article explains that schools all over the country have received lower than expected GCSE English results with a particular focus on the C/D borderline. The reason is that the grade boundaries for Controlled Assessments – the teacher-marked coursework – had dropped by 4 marks compared to last year. In other words, if a teacher had awarded a piece of controlled assessment a mark of 40 last year, it would have got a C. But if they awarded the same mark this year, thinking the grade would be pretty much the same, they would be sorely mistaken; the candidate would actually have needed a mark of 44 to get a C.

There is never any guarantee that grade boundaries will stay the same from year to year. It's the nature of exams that they change depending on how well the cohort have done. But for years previously they had stayed broadly similar, so there was also a reasonable expectation that there wouldn't be significant movement.

I was able to present the newspaper article to the head, and show him that our results were part of a much wider trend and – to a certain extent – beyond our control. He was understanding and supportive and reasonable. But none of that helps the kids who – through no fault of their own – had to enter the next stage of their lives without the GCSE English pass grade which they deserved. It feels grossly unfair.

Ask, Ask, Swap

In a bid to combat the stigma against lower sets, I've introduced a system I've seen work at other schools. The idea is that the kids who struggle the most will go into a class with two English teachers who will team-teach them. There'll also be two teaching assistants so the pupils will receive intense support to try to boost their confidence and their grades. We call them the 'super sets'. It's possible to do it at a neutral staffing cost by increasing slightly the class sizes of the top and middle sets.

I am teaching a super set of glorious but slightly odd characters with Anna, one of life's natural teachers. We take it in turns to lead the lessons, with the other one helping out, so in this particular lesson I'm milling around at the back of the room supporting her as best I can. She has planned a game to get the kids up, out of their seats and revising some key facts about the poems we have been studying lately.

The game Anna has designed is named 'Ask, ask, swap'. It should be utterly foolproof – the key instructions of the game are enshrined in its name. But, ever one for a belt-and-braces approach, Anna has made a PowerPoint to support the delivery of the game instructions.

Each child is to have a card with a question written on it. The question relates to the poems we have been studying. Each student is to walk around the classroom and pair up with another. They take it in turns to ask each other their questions and respond, and then they swap cards and repeat.

The name of the game is 'Ask ask swap', Anna says once again. 'Mr Wilson and I will now demonstrate how the game is played,' she tells the class. This is belt, braces and an extra belt.

We dutifully ask each other the questions …

'Miss Jones, how did Robert Browning present the Duke in "My Last Duchess" as controlling?'

'Mr Wilson, what point do you think Tennyson was making in "Charge of the Light Brigade"?'

The moment of truth arrives when we see whether Anna's meticulous planning has paid off. 'Mr Wilson and I have both asked each other questions. What do you think we do next? Remember that the game is called "Ask, ask, swap".'

Silence.

One hand goes up. The boy it is attached to responds by saying sincerely, 'Do you kiss?' You could tell from his voice that he wasn't taking the mick; he genuinely thought that might be the right answer. And the worst bit – no one else really laughs.

Anna manages to repress her own laughter enough to explain the rules of the game yet again.

Marking

When I was at school as a pupil, it seemed that marking often consisted of putting some random ticks on a piece of work, and writing 'Good' at the end of it. Or sometimes 'Very good'. And occasionally 'Could be better'. I clearly remember one teacher who marked so quickly that his ticks were all connected the whole way down the page; he hadn't even taken the time to lift his pen off the paper.

At some point between then and now, someone somewhere has noticed marking like that isn't tremendously helpful, and doesn't give the recipient much sense of how they can improve. And rather than respond in a measured way, they have dragged the pendulum right to the other extreme. Marking these days involves setting specific targets. Fair enough. Some schools require you to write WWW (What went well) and EBI (Even better if) on every piece of work and add some comments which will help the student know what they could do differently next time.

But it doesn't end there. The latest initiative is that every child should produce a written response to every target, demonstrating that they can now do the thing you were suggesting. So if you've said, 'EBI you use an original simile in your writing,' they're supposed to write underneath that, 'I was as excited as a bear seeing its lunch,' and you're expected to collect the work back in and confirm that they have now done that thing. The net result is that you are looking at each piece of work twice.

Then there is the question of how closely each should be marked. Clearly half-termly assessments need to be marked in detail, but when you have six, seven, eight or more classes, that is no mean feat, especially if you have to look at them twice. Homework too needs attention and, according to senior management teams, should also be marked in detail. And, just for the sake of completeness, the directive has come from the powers-that-be that all work students do in class in their exercise books should also be marked, every fortnight at a minimum.

So, to summarise, every single piece of work a child produces is to be marked by the teacher. The leadership in many schools say that day-to-day classwork in students' exercise books can be 'acknowledged' rather than marked in detail – the so-called 'tick and flick' approach. The small but not insignificant question raised by this pronouncement is 'Why?' Does anyone really, in their heart of hearts, believe that it serves the interests of any child to have teachers leafing through several hundred exercise books every fortnight and ticking every page just to acknowledge that they have been glanced at? Rather than using that time, say, planning lessons or creating resources?

The answer, of course, is that nobody really thinks that. The reason they insist on it – seemingly the *only* reason they insist on it – is because they think it will look more thorough when Ofsted show up and have a look at exercise books.

That's also why senior managers in schools have taken to popping into classrooms and having a look through some of the kids' exercise books at random, and why they ask some students to bring all their exercise books to a meeting where they will be scrutinised. Any teacher who is found wanting can expect a talking-to.

Everyone knows that marking comes with the territory for teachers. But teachers might teach anything between two hundred and four hundred students. That's a hell of a lot of classwork they are expected to 'acknowledgement mark', in addition to marking regular homeworks and half-termly assessments in detail. Sure, lessons may end at 3.30, but a lot of days there are meetings after school. And even if there aren't, this is the time they have in the school day to get to the photocopier or write their reports or follow up incidents that have happened during the day or plan lessons. It's just not a reasonable expectation, and how can the marking be anything other than cursory when it needs to be done in that volume?

Such policies are not uncommon in state schools. The most galling thing is that it doesn't appear to spring from any desire to actually help students improve in their work. Its motivation is entirely to appease or impress inspectors who will be looking for evidence to support their grading of a school. That seems to be the ultimate goal behind more and more decrees. And the end result is that much of the marking is as unhelpful as it was in my day. It's all a bit demoralising.

Nice To Meet You

Teaching has taught me that I have poorer than average facial recognition. Where most of my colleagues can name the kids in their class after a few weeks or a month at most, I find it a real challenge. I need to sit down and study seating plans, and tend to attach a name to a particular desk rather than a particular face, meaning that I'm much less good at recognising pupils I teach when I encounter them somewhere out of the ordinary.

A little gentle research has informed me that the inability to recognise faces is called prosopagnosia. In its most severe form sufferers might not be able to recognise the faces of their loved ones, or even their own face. Clearly mine is a very mild version, but when I reflect on it I do realise that I seem to spend a lot of time outside school holding out my hand and saying, 'Nice to meet you,' to people, only for them to furrow their brow and say in a hesitant tone, 'But we met a couple of weeks ago,' while they confusedly grip my hand. Thinking back on it I've also noticed it from time to time at the theatre: I sometimes can't tell whether we have met a character before or if this is their first appearance. All in all it's a hindrance for a teacher who has to teach several hundred children every year.

One particular situation involving former students highlights the difficulty. I am back in Cambridge for the wedding of two former colleagues. They have hired a village hall for their reception, and every moment of the day is a joy. Or nearly every moment. The issue arises with the waiters and waitresses. The couple have asked former students to do the job. Inevitably, I don't recognise a single one. That's not an issue until one young woman who is kindly collecting a glass says, 'Ah, Mr Wilson. How are you?' In the split second I have to plan my response, I choose an option I often go for in such circumstances: try to style it out. 'Ah, HELLO. It's lovely to see you. What are you up to these days?' tends to cover it. Only on this occasion she says, 'Oh, thank goodness for that. I was *petrified* that you wouldn't remember who I was.' She laughs and I join in, laughing harder and harder in an attempt to convey what an utterly preposterous suggestion that is.

Hampstead Heath

Zoe comes to visit and we go for long walk on Hampstead Heath. It's a cold, bright autumn day and we're passing the swimming ponds and she's telling me that her doctors are really happy with how her treatment is progressing, and that to all intents and purposes she is cancer free. In the background there are the squeals and gasps of people tentatively dipping their toes into the ice-cold water.

Her relationship with Dan is going from strength to strength. He has proposed, and they are getting married next year. The news could not be any better and Zoe is over the moon. We walk on arm in arm, with the sun shining and surrounded by the distant noises of splashing and laughter and children playing.

Of Mice and Men

Few things beat the sheer pleasure of introducing students to a great story, and seeing them become enraptured by it. But teaching books isn't just about entertainment; heaven forfend that joy should be a reason for doing something. Books also teach children about life, about right and wrong, about how to be a good person. As we discuss the moral dilemmas that characters face, so we discuss how they should face difficult choices in their lives.

I have by now taught all sorts of books from Chaucer and Shakespeare right up to contemporary fiction. I have enjoyed teaching all of them (more or less - if I'm honest Jane Austen can take a hike). But there's one which really stands out, partly because I've taught it more than any other, but mostly because of the effect it has on classes young and old, across all levels of ability. That book is *Of Mice and Men* by John Steinbeck.

Which is why it's particularly upsetting when Michael Gove decides that British children should study only British literature. Suddenly Dickens, Shelley and the Brontës are in, and Steinbeck, Salinger and Harper Lee are out.

The government was concerned that up to 90 per cent of young people study *Of Mice and Men*. It's worth taking a moment to actually think about that. With all the urgent problems in society, with all the homelessness and poverty and suffering, the government was worried that too many children were studying a great book.

A book that is short but so intricately constructed that you can teach kids everything you'd want them to know about literature through it. Its themes cut across the decades to speak to the children of today; hope, loyalty and friendship are as important now as they were then. And for kids from disadvantaged or troubled backgrounds, the idea of choosing to believe that a better life lies within reach is profound and vital.

Even the most streetwise of teenagers is gripped by the story of two friends from California in the Great Depression of the 1930s, and their desire to follow their dream to forge a better life for themselves. They feel sorry for Lennie, the pleasant farm labourer with a mental disability, when he is bullied by Curley. They ridicule Curley's wife, so unimportant that she is denied a name of her own, and condemn her sexuality, before they realise that her confident and flirtatious exterior belies her true fragility and insecurity. They recoil at the racist treatment of Crooks, the stable buck who is outcast for the colour of his skin. They love the fact there's some swearing. And every single time, the ending brings the house down.

The book is well suited to the syllabus. The language and symbolism are clear and beautifully handled. The plot grips them. But more than any of that, students learn that, like the characters in the book, people are often more complex than they appear. And they will come across weak and vulnerable members of society, social outcasts and people who give off a poor first impression. Maybe next time they do, they'll think of Lennie and Curley's wife and Crooks and give people the benefit of the doubt.

It's the classroom conversations that the novel sparks which are where the gold dust lies. Students who have hitherto mostly scowled or rolled their eyes or slept in class, suddenly have passionate views on what it means to be a good friend, or where the limits of loyalty lie. They hold court on how you should deal with bullies, or describe their own experiences of how ethnic minorities are still ostracised in today's society.

The reality is that some of these students won't read many more books in their lives, but at least they've experienced what it is to really enjoy a good story, and to allow it to shine a light on their own lives.

Yes, *Of Mice and Men* has been a staple of English departments for ages. I can pretty much recite it. But there's a reason for that and it's new to each cohort of students who study it. And yes, there are other books which are also great, and yes, we can always find a way to work Steinbeck into some other part of the curriculum, and yes, change is inevitable and probably good. But it's still sad that George and Lennie are banished to the back of the book cupboard for now. Some other Education Secretary will come along sooner or later and reinstate them, with a bold new message that we must broaden our children's horizons and encourage them to study foreign literature. But until then, I'll miss them.

Lunch Duty

I am on lunch duty in the canteen. The idea is that you – one human with no military training – are supposed to single-handedly stop a tide of humanity that is heading inexorably towards fish and chips, and somehow corral it into a semblance of order.

As the chaos subsides, and children filter off to tables clutching their precious nutritional cargo, two girls approach me. 'Can we ask you a question?' they say. What comes next could sound cheeky coming from other mouths. I can only tell you that these were sweet, innocent girls who were genuinely confused.

'Is the heart part of the reproductive system?' they ask, and look at me with wide-eyed inquisitiveness. It takes me a few seconds to realise that they are being totally serious. 'We've been revising our biology and keep getting confused.'

I tell them that actually it's part of the circulatory system. And as they walk away, satisfied with the answer, I'm left pondering whether that might be the most profound question ever asked about human relationships.

The U-Turn

As I sit at my desk mourning the decision to remove *Of Mice and Men* from the GCSE curriculum I get to thinking about the role of the state in education. As a state school teacher, even – and perhaps especially as head teacher – you operate at the whim of the government. The Education Secretary sets the parameters of what you can and can't do, where you should focus, how your success or otherwise will be judged. But it's a very problematic arrangement.

One of the issues is that every new Education Secretary wants to put their stamp on the school system. The work of their predecessors is often stopped in its tracks and replaced with their own pet projects. So continuity and joined-up thinking are in short supply.

The education system is littered with examples of massive U-turns. For years students were allowed to take modular exams because that was seen as a fairer way of assessing them. Then one day modules were blamed for dumbing down assessment and kicked to the kerb. When I started out, arts subjects were seen as valuable for developing the whole student and promoting self-expression. Then they were relegated to playing a less significant role than some subjects that are seen as 'more academic'. Coursework was a valuable part of a holistic learning experience, and then it was too open to exploitation and scrapped. I could go on and on.

These U-turns can cause carnage in schools that is further exacerbated by the amount of time new decisions take to trickle through. The changes in the GCSE grading system are a good example. Michael Gove decided to change from an A*–G range to 9–1 in 2013. It took years for the change to actually happen. When it eventually came into force, and it caused – to put it mildly – teething problems, he was long gone from the Department for Education. A new government and a new team inherited this initiative, but didn't own it, didn't really care about it, and in any case were busy charting a different course for themselves.

The saddest thing is that what's at stake here is nothing less than the experience our children have at school and beyond – what qualifications they will get, what jobs they will find, even what sort of people they will become. And it's students and their families who end up worse off for this lack of continuity. Somehow I'm supposed to explain to a group of Year 10s and their parents that they will receive a numbered grade for their GCSE in English and maths as they are the first subjects to move to the new system, but a lettered grade in all their other subjects. So a child could have as their GCSE results 3 Bs, 3 Cs, a 6, an A and a 4.

You can imagine how the conversations with parents go. 'Yes, I agree it does seem a little unusual. And I know that your younger child is assessed against National Curriculum levels, but no, actually that's an entirely different numerical scale from GCSE grades. It is confusing, yes, and I agree it's going to be difficult for employers to understand.'

Surely the education of our children should not be subject to the whim of whoever walks into the Secretary of State's office? How about a cross-party committee of elected MPs to set long-term education policy for our country? They could oversee learning for everyone from preschoolers up to nineteen-year-olds and offer stable, coherent planning. And above all else, get some teachers on that committee, and not just career politicians.

This fanciful vision is the product of a long day. It's about as likely to ever exist as I am to find Narnia at the back of my wardrobe. But there's no harm in dreaming.

Poetry Live

Every year the exam board organises the sort of event which would be utter bliss if you were fortunate enough to be going alone, or perhaps with a friend. Named 'GCSE Poetry Live', it sees renowned poets reading their work aloud, commenting on some of the circumstances that led them to write the poems, and taking questions from the audience. On a Sunday afternoon with a crisp glass of white and the company of your fellow adults? Delightful. On a wet Tuesday morning in November with one hundred teenagers in tow? Purgatory itself.

As we arrive outside the Royal Festival Hall with our merry band of budding poets, it becomes immediately clear that we stand out. Lined up in military straight rows are hundreds of students from several private schools. Their uniforms are immaculate. Their hair is all perfectly coiffed. I'm not quite sure whether they are actually clutching anthologies of poetry and reciting them to each other enthusiastically, but if not, that's the aura they give off. I look back at our rabble. Their shirts are universally untucked. They are making a noise roughly akin to a football stadium when a goal has gone the wrong way, and somewhere at the back of the line a boy is kicking his classmate in the nuts. It's going to be a long day.

We all head into the hall and take our seats to listen to Carol Ann Duffy, not to be confused with Margaret Thatcher, reciting some of her poetry. Everyone claps politely. She asks whether anyone has any questions they would like to ask. One of the immaculately uniformed, coiffed-hair boys is standing at the microphone.

'Yah', he says, 'thanks for taking my question. I was wondering to what extent you think that memory is a reconstructive force?'

A murmur of approval goes round the hall, and Duffy responds with a considered and nuanced answer. But I miss the end of it because, to my horror, I see one of our worst-behaved boys is standing at the microphone, waiting to ask his question next. I try to gesture to a nearby teacher to get him to sit down, but I'm too late; the spotlight is already shining on his untucked shirt.

As the light gets in his eyes, he says into the microphone, 'Oh, for fffffffuc–' The incomplete word echoes around the Royal Festival Hall. And then he is asking his question: 'Is it true that you ... like ... write about your feelings?'

I feel a bit sorry for the Poet Laureate. First she has her poem pulped because of a complaint from an over-zealous exam invigilator and now this. But in fairness to her, she answers the question thoughtfully and at length, and on reflection I'm glad that our dishevelled boy got to ask his question. Poetry, after all, belongs as much to our kids as it does the kids from any private school, no matter how posh. As we traipse, a merry band, back towards Waterloo station, I overhear one boy asking whether it's the Thames we're walking past. He lives in this city but has never seen the river before; this is a fourteen-year-old child who hasn't been into central London.

It's a reminder that many of the kids we teach live not only in physical poverty but in cultural poverty too. I wonder how old the kids with the coiffed hair were when their parents first took them to the Tate Modern on the banks of the river, or to the Science Museum or the West End. But still, it would be nice if ours tucked their shirts in when requested.

Senior Leadership

I have been asked to take on an assistant head role. It's a step up from head of department and a step below deputy head, and is the most junior of the senior leadership positions. It means that I'll line-manage a few heads of department, a head of year, and take on responsibility for the some of the school's strategic priorities. One of them is 'achievement' – a single word on a job description but, it strikes me, quite a big thing to take charge of when it comes to managing a school.

I needn't worry, I am told, because the school has signed up for some kind of support network to help us lead it towards the highest academic standards. At the centre of this scheme are meetings which take place in a very grand hall in the centre of London.

As I arrive for my first meeting I am struck by the fact that this is unlike any other teaching meeting I have ever been to. Usually they are held in a dingy classroom after hours, where chewing gum from the underside of the desks surgically attaches itself to your trousers and pictures of penises stare back at you from desks that are too low. You're offered coffee that the canteen ladies made before they left several hours ago and stuck in a flask and, if you're lucky, you get an apology for the lack of milk and a broken plain digestive to go with it.

But here there is fancy lighting and professional projection. There are proper pastries and a top-notch lunch. And there are hundreds of teachers. These meetings are a Very Big Deal. They have something of the evangelical zeal of the old-fashioned revival meeting about them.

There is a charismatic leader who addresses his flock with the fervour of a preacher. He exhorts them to do everything they can to make their schools' results better and better and better. He reminds them that it is their moral duty to do so. And he employs the language of medicine to help hammer home his point: you need to analyse the results you got last year to work out where there is sickness. You need to diagnose the problems. And you need to put treatment in place.

He doesn't quite offer to lay his hands on you so that the scales may fall from your eyes and your sickness retreat from your body, although at times it feels as if that might be coming. Instead he introduces a series of colleagues who share their tricks and tips for how to get your results up.

Let's be clear: wanting to raise standards is good. Having the energy to gather people together and share some proven teaching strategies is good. It's the next bit which doesn't sit well. In fact, it gets to the very nub of everything that I believe is wrong with our education system at the moment.

One of the speakers starts to describe qualifications that schools can teach pupils very quickly, even in the last few weeks of the academic year, and that count towards a school's overall statistics. Another describes how she has experimented with different exam boards and found the one which gives the highest number of top grades. Yet another tells of a loophole in the way schools' achievements are calculated which means that you can enter pupils for a particular GCSE exam, NOT TEACH THEM ANYTHING ABOUT IT, and it will benefit the stats. The child concerned has to go into the exam hall, write their candidate number and centre number on the paper, doodle for an hour or so, and then they can leave. They get absolutely nothing from it, but it will boost the school's numbers. And people are scribbling this down. And they tell me that they've done it: entered pupils for an exam they haven't been prepared for.

My feeling as I leave my first meeting is that a lot of the advice crossed the line into gaming, plotting tactics, trying to exploit loopholes just to massage the numbers. They claim everything they do has a moral purpose because it gets kids good grades and that improves their life chances. But there is more to life than grades, and I'm sorry but entering children for qualifications you haven't even taught them is immoral.

The enthusiasm of the teachers attending, I reflected, was not because they loved doing these things either, but because they were under such enormous, crippling pressure from Ofsted to produce ever higher results. And here was an organisation that would tell them exactly how they could do that. If they weren't members, they'd be missing out on all those tips and tricks. The enthusiasm was relief that they could do something to protect their schools from impossible expectations. But none of this is what I went into teaching to do and I travel home feeling disillusioned and pretty despondent.

Drawing Conclusions

I am marking some assessments from my Year 10s. They had to read a short murder mystery story and answer a few questions testing their comprehension. In the story, one of the key suspects is described as shifting awkwardly from foot to foot, and sweating profusely as he is questioned. The students were asked what conclusions they could draw from his behaviour. Most are able to talk about how he seems uncomfortable, nervous when put under pressure, and how the author may be trying to imply his guilt.

One girl has turned the page on its side and drawn a number of stick figures. One has beads of sweat dripping from his head and a large arrow pointing at him saying, 'He did it.' It takes me a while to realise that she has interpreted the question literally and drawn her conclusions. It makes my day.

Gove Again

Let's return to your friend and mine, one Michael Andrew Gove. During his tenure as Secretary of State, he made a number of changes to the way grammar is taught in schools. Let me start by giving him a little credit.

I think he was right that there needed to be more of a focus on the basics of spelling, punctuation and grammar in the English curriculum. For too long they had been neglected in favour of things like reading comprehension and creative writing. That is not to underplay the vital importance of those things. But it's hard to do either of them well without a solid understanding of how writing works. And I agree with him that we are doing children, particularly disadvantaged children, a disservice sending them out into the world with sub-par writing skills.

As is so often the case, though, poor implementation turns a good idea into an out-and-out joke. The government's first error was to create a special new test just for spelling, punctuation and grammar. It was introduced for ten- and eleven-year-olds in their last year of primary school as part of the SATs. SAT is short for standard assessment tests. They actually haven't been called that for years – they're now known as National Curriculum tests – but for some reason the name has stuck. As things stand, they are taken in Key Stage 1 when kids are about seven (tests! At seven!) and in Key Stage 2 when they are about ten.

The government like tests because they create data and ways of keeping tabs on teachers. Never mind that they are another burden for children whose final year in primary school is already consumed with exam preparation.

They also made the content way too complex. I mean, absurdly so. Kids are expected to be able to identify something called a 'fronted adverbial'. Somehow I managed to get through A level English, an English degree and a qualification in teaching English without having even heard of the concept of a fronted adverbial, let alone being able to spot one. The National Curriculum offers a definition: a fronted adverbial is 'a word or phrase that is used, like an adverb, to modify a verb or clause and has been moved in front of the verb or clause'. So that's cleared that up.

But it's even worse than that. Although the pupils take this exam at the end of their time in primary school, the national curriculum actually requires that children be able to understand fronted adverbials from Year 4. Subordinate clauses should be known and labelled correctly from the age of seven, 'determiners' come in at age eight, and you're the grand old age of nine before you're expected to know about modal verbs and relative clauses. I can't imagine trying to teach that to younger children.

This nonsensical focus on terminology – as distinct from actual, useful guidance on how to write well – would be comic if it weren't so awful. Think of Sean who once produced a piece of coursework from his shoe. Does he need to know how to label a subordinate clause or a determiner? No, he needs to focus on capital letters and full stops.

The upshot for us in secondary schools is that pupils arrive armed with a vast, if rather superficial and often insecure, knowledge of relatively obscure grammatical language. They have heard terms that their English teachers barely know, but there isn't much feeling among the colleagues I've spoken to that their writing has improved.

Was Michael Gove a particularly bad Education Secretary? I think he was just more proactive than some of his immediate predecessors and successors. Most seem content to keep things ticking over and are therefore fairly benign if rather ineffective. But Gove was a man determined to make dramatic changes, with seemingly little interest in the opinions or experiences of teachers. He was only in his post four years but we are still feeling the effects of his tenure. He is a prime example of the havoc that a political appointee can wreak on the lives of students, teachers and the health and stability of our national education system.

Wedding

Zoe is married in a beautiful hotel in Cambridgeshire. It's a small ceremony, full of love and poetry and family. Zoe and Dan are on wonderful form and barely stop smiling all day. They have hired a magician to wander around the reception and Zoe and I gasp as he makes a card we have chosen appear in the wallet which has been in my pocket the whole time. At the service, I am honoured to give a reading from Victor Hugo's *Les Misérables*:

You can give without loving, but you can never love without giving. The great acts of love are done by those who are habitually performing small acts of kindness. We pardon to the extent that we love. Love is knowing that even when you are alone, you will never be lonely again. And the great happiness of life is the conviction that we are loved. Loved for ourselves. And even loved in spite of ourselves.

Safe Sex

Rachel the drama teacher is telling us about her morning. She had to sit at the back of a classroom while her Year 10 form had a special sex education session, delivered by an outside agency. The speaker did a great job outlining the risks of unsafe sex. As he drew his talk to a close he told them, 'At the end of the day there is only one way you can be one hundred per cent sure of avoiding unwanted pregnancies or STIs. And the only way that you can be certain is through something called [*dramatic pause*] abstinence. Does anybody know what abstinence is?'

There was a long period of silence, followed by some muffled discussions on tables. A single hand went up. The boy it belonged to is sincere and sweet – he was not playing for laughs. In his mind he had been puzzling out what the only way you can avoid STIs or unwanted pregnancies might be. And he was ready to announce his findings.

'Is it when the man puts his penis in the woman's ear?'

Rachel allowed herself a little laugh, assuming it would be absorbed into the general laughter of the room. Wrong. The rest of the class heard this answer and judged it to be reasonable. One can only feel sympathy for any girlfriend this young man might have had. If she were to announce that she would like to practise abstinence she would have found that she was in for a nasty surprise.

Exam Mania

It's exam season again, and seeing it this year from a manage-ment position I notice how, as a school, we actually come pretty close to losing our collective mind. Clearly everyone in the building is under pressure for the results to be good – from the head to heads of department and individual teachers. But you'd like to think that we could model for students how to deal with pressure in a way that is propor-tionate, measured and calm. Reader, we do not.

Teachers are encouraged, directed and nudged into providing extra provision for their classes. This comes in all sorts of guises: after-school revision sessions, Easter holiday classes, breakfast clubs, targeted interventions, catch-up classes, take-out groups and Saturday schools. Quite often pupils are told that these sessions are compulsory. They get home after a long day at school to find letters telling them they'll have to give up their supposedly free time to go in and do more work in school. The only time the kids are left alone is overnight, and to be honest it feels like it won't be long before someone suggests that we should organise revi-sion sleepovers.

More or less every teacher I have worked with cares deeply about their students' achievement, and will do extra marking or find additional resources, or take time out to help support a pupil. We do it every day in our normal lessons. The problem is that all the extra fuss at this time of year actually makes it harder to do that. You end up running one-size-fits-all revision classes for lots of kids who don't need or want them, meaning you don't have much or any time to provide that extra support for the individual kids, particularly in non-exam classes, who desperately need it.

What sort of message does our exam mania send out about learning? From where I'm standing it communicates that last-minute cramming is a good way of studying. It also unsettles the pupils: as the requests for them to come to out-of-hours sessions ratchet up in frequency and urgency, they can sense the nerves of their teachers.

I have spent many a Saturday morning sitting in my classroom with past papers ready to go. But quite a few of the kids who have been told to come vote with their feet and stay away. It's hard to blame them. They have done a full week in school already plus homework. I taught them the stuff perfectly well first time around. Why should they give up their weekend to hear it again? Can you imagine if someone in a normal adult workplace suggested all staff should come in on Saturday mornings to redo some work they had already done? There would be mutiny.

There's also a massive irony here. Two of the words we use over and over in assemblies with kids are 'resilience' and 'motivation'. We talk about the importance of them taking responsibility for their own learning. But we don't trust them enough to actually let them do that. So we perpetuate their dependence on teachers, and they arrive at university or college or the workplace without having had to work independently before.

As a school leader I am now, of course, involved in encouraging colleagues to run these sessions, and it leaves me deeply uncomfortable. If it were up to me I would leave the kids to their study leave, and of course be available for help, support and advice whenever needed. There might be some kids who would genuinely benefit from more structured support than that, and they should get it. But they would be the exception rather than the rule.

There's another reason I think this is all a waste of everyone's life, and it's a fairly fundamental one: it doesn't seem to work. I occasionally try to make this point in leadership meetings, but from the facial expressions it generates, I might as well have announced that I think we should open a school on Venus. All these extra sessions reassure leaders that we are Doing Something. But the year we did the most extra intervention was the year that results were lowest across the school.

I can only speculate as to why that might be, but if you spread staff that thinly I'd say it's inevitable that they will teach worse lessons. And the kids are just knackered. Rather than arriving at the start of the exam period at their academic peak and ready to show off everything they have learned, they are instead under-rested, demoralised and overloaded. No one, not even the real keen beans, can keep up that level of focus and attention over weeks and weeks.

Sociologists talk about the curriculum that students study at school – maths, English, science and so on – and the hidden curriculum. The hidden curriculum is the other things they learn, that aren't written down in any specification: how to interact with others, how to plan their time effectively, that actions have consequences and so on.

That's why part of the teacher's role is to model how to approach life in its broadest terms; how to deal with conflict, how to treat people well and, yes, how to deal with pressure. If the adults in the room can't be measured and unpanicked, what hope do those in our charge have?

Thank You

I have a Year 9 group who are pretty challenging. They're not particularly badly behaved; they're just so loud. I reckon my voice projects quite well but even getting them to hear my futile requests for quiet is tricky. If I'm honest, what flusters me most is that I feel I should be able to control them better. Here I am dishing out advice to others about what they could do differently to improve their lessons while it sounds as though there is a World Cup final going on in my own. I dread any other teacher coming to the door and seeing it all.

It's in this context, and on a day when they are especially excitable, that I notice through the window in the classroom door that one of my Year 11 boys is loitering outside. He is a bit of a wannabe class clown; he has the confidence to heckle and interrupt lessons, but is not quite switched on enough to have anything funny to say, so the result is that more of the class are eye-rolling than laughing.

He is waving and doing something I think is meant to be a dance. I decide to deploy that greatest strategy again and tactically ignore him. In any case I am busy doing my own semi-dance in an effort to get the class to pay attention to me. But he keeps going. The class are noticing and the volume, which was already ratcheted up to what I thought was its maximum, finds a new peak. There's nothing else for it. I throw the door open, rather flustered, and launch into a tirade. 'Mark! Can't you see I'm busy? I don't need you trying to be funny outside my classroom door, do I?'

A pause. Mark is uncharacteristically quiet. 'I just came along to say thank you for teaching me. And I was waving to get your attention because I wanted to give you this.' From his bag, Mark pulls a box of chocolates. It's a box of chocolates which has seen better days. I can imagine him buying it a few days previously and shoving it deep into his school bag, before that same bag is used as a makeshift goalpost at break time and sustains a few kicks, and is then slung around the school bus a fair bit before it sees the light of day again in this moment. But it is very sweet and I immediately feel bad for having a go at him.

'Thank you, Mark,' I manage to say, 'that's very kind of you.' But I haven't quite changed my tone of voice from frustrated to grateful yet, so it comes out a little more aggressively than I intend. He smiles, waves and is gone and I feel incredibly touched. But only briefly, because the roar of Year 9 can be ignored no longer.

Complaint

A parent has made a serious complaint about a teacher on my team called Toyah. Toyah is diligent and caring and a great teacher. I've watched several of her classes, and seen first-hand how carefully she plans her lessons, and how she deals with students – polite, calm, firm but fair.

The complaint is typed and runs to several pages. The parent explains that their stepdaughter, Jasmine, has been left 'traumatised' following an incident which took place in Toyah's lesson the previous week. Jasmine was accused by Toyah of cheating in an assessment which would count towards her final grade. Jasmine, the letter goes on, would never dream of cheating. She is hard-working and diligent and such an accusation is a stain on her character.

Jasmine's stepfather also explains that, having discovered the alleged cheating, Toyah tore up Jasmine's coursework in front of the rest of the class, a humiliation which left her with extreme stress. Jasmine was told that she would have to complete the coursework again after school and under supervision. This was an injustice which could not be ignored.

Toyah's outburst of 'uncontrolled rage and violence' is, according to Jasmine's stepdad, evidence that she is 'entirely unsuitable to work with children' and, with a dramatic flourish, he states that he has 'sought legal advice in connection with the incident'.

But Jasmine's stepfather is not yet done with his catalogue of rage. He also says he tried to raise the issue with Toyah at parents' evening a couple of weeks later and was told that they could not discuss it. In his eyes this was outrage on outrage. The travesty is so heinous, he concludes, that he demands an urgent meeting with Toyah's line manager and the head teacher.

I am already familiar with the saga because Toyah came to talk to me about it after the parents' evening, but I heard a rather different version of events. Paul asks me to look into it and come back to him with some facts about what happened that we can share with Jasmine's stepdad in the meeting.

I meet with Toyah and give her every reassurance I can that I will support her, but I know from my own experience that allegations like this are always difficult.

Then I set about trying to put together some evidence. People often say that teaching is an amalgamation of many different jobs; you're a counsellor, a psychologist, a judge, an administrator and a life coach. Some days you're also a negotiator, an advocate and a nurse. Today I can add police investigator to the list.

First there is the cheating allegation. Toyah says that she tore up two matching pieces of coursework – Jasmine's and that of the girl she was sitting beside. The other girl, by the way, thought this was a fair cop and accepted her punishment, as did her family. And not to put too fine a point on it, knowing the students involved, I think it is unlikely that the other girl copied from Jasmine.

After ripping up their work Toyah wisely kept the remnants. She hadn't shredded the pages into oblivion – she had just torn them once down the middle. Therefore we could piece them back together, and it was clear that they were word for word the same. So it was impossible to deny the charges of copying.

Then there's the issue of the parents' evening, and the allegation that Toyah shut down the conversation with Jasmine's parents. Other teachers present confirmed Toyah's account that she gave an accurate assessment of Jasmine's progress and suggested ways that she could improve further in English lessons. That took about five minutes, which is the amount of time each parent is allocated.

When Jasmine's stepdad brought up the cheating issue at the end of the conversation, Toyah had a queue of other parents waiting to see her. She politely told him that they were out of time and that he'd have to make another arrangement to see her if they wanted to discuss the cheating. On being told this, Jasmine's stepdad became aggressive, raising his voice, and had to be asked by another teacher to leave the room.

Armed with this information, Paul and I invite Jasmine's parents into his office for the angrily requested meeting. 'Thanks for coming in today and for taking the time to write such a detailed letter,' Paul begins. The first sting comes in the next sentence. 'Maybe we could start with your statement that you have sought legal advice on this matter. Please could you tell me which solicitor has agreed to take this case on?' Jasmine's stepdad opens his mouth and then closes it again. He stutters.

'Just give me the name of the solicitor who is advising you, if you would,' Paul continues. They splutter and delay under his direct gaze. After an agonising thirty seconds or so Paul starts flicking through the original letter and says, 'Well, we've established that was a lie – let's see what else we've got.' It is devastating and forensic and brilliant.

Over the next twenty minutes Paul explains why none of their arguments hold water. He reads out sections of Jasmine's work and the work of the girl she was sitting beside. He quotes from the exam board regulations about malpractice, and points out that Jasmine's actions could have put the credibility of the whole cohort of candidates in jeopardy. Under increasing pressure, Jasmine's parents try to suggest that there may be a racist motive for persecuting her, despite having no evidence to suggest any such claim and Toyah being black herself, and Paul tells them that if they insinuate that again he will ask them to leave. And when Jasmine's stepdad admits under questioning that he raised his voice and loured over Toyah at the parents' evening, Paul asks why he shouldn't ban him from the school site for aggressive and intimidating behaviour towards staff.

Jasmine's parents leave with their tails between their legs having admitted that their daughter probably did cheat, and that the stepfather acted aggressively. Paul follows the meeting up with a letter home in which he quotes chapter and verse of the law which gives him the authority to ban parents from the school site for behaviour which threatens the safety of members of the school community, which he subsequently does. I meet with Toyah straight afterwards and reassure her that she has nothing to worry about, and that the matter will now be closed. She visibly relaxes.

As I reflect on it on my way home, I wonder about the tearing up of the coursework in front of the class. Was it the best way to deal with the situation? On balance and with hindsight it was probably a bit confrontational and it may have been better handled with a chat in private after the lesson. But it did set a clear example to the rest of the class that cheating won't be tolerated. And did it warrant the level of complaint and the aggression with which the parents pursued it? Categorically not. What do her parents' actions teach Jasmine about how to behave? If you do something wrong never admit it, just fight and threaten those in authority.

As for how Paul handled it, I have never seen anything like it before or since. I tell friends who teach elsewhere the story, and there is broad agreement that they would give their right hand for a head who would deal so firmly with nonsense like this. Ofsted gather the views of parents by sending them all a survey to complete, and even a few disgruntled responses can skew the data to imply dissatisfaction with the school and its management. Too many heads therefore pander to ludicrous complaints from families.

It goes without saying that parents will from time to time have legitimate complaints about staff, and they should be handled sensitively and investigated fully and action taken where required. But where the complaints are vexatious, more heads need the courage to dismiss them with the vigour that Paul showed.

Stabbing

Members of the senior leadership team are expected to wear hi-vis jackets as they walk about the corridors. The idea is that any teenagers who are up to no good will see you coming and desist in their mischief. A side effect is that you look like a prat. When I tell Zoe, she remarks that it has the advantage of hiding whatever I am wearing underneath it.

We are also issued with enormous walkie-talkies which clip to our belts and provide an intriguing hump in the outline of said hi-vis jacket which only adds to the appeal. The purpose of the walkie-talkies is so we can communicate with one another when we are out and about on duty, and so that reception can get in touch with us quickly if there is some sort of situation that needs attention.

A pretty standard message would be something like, 'This is main reception. Please could Mr Wilson head to room 205 where a teacher requires senior staff assistance.' Pretty mundane stuff.

But I am sitting in my office one day when a highly unusual call comes through. The first sound as the speaker crackles into action is just heavy breathing. About ten seconds later or so I hear one of the other assistant heads say, 'Mr Cole calling reception, please can you call 999 *immediately* and ask for the police and the ambulance.' Another pause. 'Please can—' and his voice breaks off amid the sound of shouting in the background. 'Please can all senior staff come to the front car park immediately. That's all senior staff to the front car park immediately, extremely urgent.'

It's a short journey from my office, and when I arrive I meet Mark, the colleague whose voice I had heard on the walkie-talkie. His hi-vis jacket is streaked with blood. There is blood on his hands and down his arms. 'He's been stabbed,' he says, pointing at a kid lying conscious on the ground, trousers ripped at the lower leg, and the blood trickling down the concrete surface next to him.

Within a few seconds there are what seems like dozens of staff on the scene, some tending to the boy, some restraining the apparent perpetrator, others directing the police. I don't know either of the boys involved and busy myself by moving on the crowds of spectators that are beginning to gather. It's a grim day and part of a growing pattern of knife crime across the capital.

Recruitment

We are advertising for a new English teacher to join the team. It's a good school, and the salary includes financial weighting for working in inner London, so on paper it should be an attractive position.

A couple of days after applications have closed I go and visit the HR office to collect the folder of applications. It feels notably thin in my hand. I open it back in my office and find two lonely applications. A quick scan of the first tells me it is from someone who is working as a traffic warden and has no teacher training or experience. The other candidate has misspelt the word 'teacher' in the box where they note down the position they are applying for.

It's a shame there is so little interest in the position but I can't honestly blame people for not wanting this to be their life.

Coursework

Not content with getting rid of American texts from the English literature syllabus, changing the grading system and introducing bemused children to the concept of fronted adverbials, Michael Gove has also done away with coursework.

When I first started teaching, we'd have lovely afternoons talking about creative writing. The kids would spend two or three weeks honing their work. Every day in class we would read some brilliant literature: a really descriptive passage from Dickens or Eliot or even David Walliams, whatever had caught my eye that day. We'd talk about what made it so effective. Was it the sentence structure or the use of adjectives or the sensory language or the humour? After we'd talked about it they would redraft their own work, experimenting with different techniques, and by the end of the process they often had impressive pieces of writing that they were proud of, and which frequently read like actual grown-up writing rather than the words of schoolchildren.

I would mark their work, and I would swap some samples with other teachers on the team to make sure that we were all marking to the same level and adjust our marks as necessary if we weren't. We'd also send a sample off to the exam board for someone completely external to check that there was no funny business with the marking. And those coursework marks would count as 40 per cent of students' final marks for their GCSE, the rest coming from exams at the end of the course.

It meant that the majority of the assessment was still external, but kids who didn't work well under time pressure, or who had had a bad day or some sort of trauma around exam time weren't too heavily penalised. They still stood a chance of getting the pass grade in English which would open the door to sixth form or college or any number of other ambitions which require a pass in GCSE English.

There were concerns, though, that this system wasn't fair. Some children get more help than others at home, so the complaints went, and there was always a fear that unscrupulous teachers would be tempted to provide too much support, such that it became impossible to say that a student's work was truly their own. So they cracked down on coursework, and rebranded it as 'controlled assessment'. Students weren't allowed to work on their projects at home any more; it all had to be done in class and under teacher supervision. They could draft and redraft but without receiving feedback in between times. It wasn't the free and creative process it had once been. And because it was marked by teachers, the mutterings that some teachers somewhere were abusing the system continued.

So Gove just got rid of the whole shebang. No coursework, no controlled assessment, just exams. When I first started teaching, kids could get some marks towards their final grade for speaking and listening; it would encourage and reward those who could give great speeches or formulate a coherent and reasoned argument or lead constructive and inclusive group discussions. That was all removed from the main qualification too.

Kieron was among the many students who would have been disadvantaged had this happened during his GCSE course. His writing wasn't the strongest, and he struggled with getting his thoughts down on paper. But he could express himself orally with clarity and precision, and he was rewarded for that. It wasn't enough to get him to a magic C grade, but it got him a D rather than an E. The point is that he was rewarded for skills beyond being able to do exams.

But now, the only means of assessment in English is four exams at the end of the course. Gove also decided, in his wisdom, that kids shouldn't take the texts in with them to the literature exams. And across many other subjects it was the same picture. Coursework and controlled assessment gone, and the stabilisers designed to support those who most need it removed. So there are now no formulae sheets in maths, and foundation tier papers – which adjusted the levels of questioning so that everyone could access the question paper – were done away with.

The word the Department for Education used for these changes was 'rigorous'. They were making assessment rigorous again, as if previously top grades had been dished out like sweets. Gove was returning the nation to the golden age of education, when exams were tough and there was no namby-pamby watering down of the curriculum. There are so many problems with this line of thinking, it's hard to know where to start.

The most fundamental is that you need to stop and think about what you actually want to assess. In my subject it's probably going to be things like how well students can understand the meaning of texts, how well they can construct their own creative or argumentative writing, the extent to which they show sensitivity in responding to literature, and their imagination. If you only have exams to do all those things, the risk is that a large proportion of what you actually assess is how good kids are at exams, how good their time management is, and how good their memory is. Now there may be merit in assessing those things, but it's not the same as assessing a child's aptitude or ability in any given subject.

I have taught plenty of kids who are amazingly creative, great writers and voracious, critical readers, but who have terrible time-management skills. In fact Amelia, who made a potentially hitherto unnoticed connection between *The Tempest* Act 3 scene 2 and *Frankenstein* only for it to be cruelly rebuffed, wasn't great at getting her thoughts down under time restrictions. The idea that she might not get the top grade is unconscionable. Under the old system at least students could be rewarded for work they had slaved over and perfected at home.

And there are those who are imaginative but struggle with technical skills, those who are insightful but have poor recall, and those who are talented but suffer from anxiety. Zofia, who gave such a moving speech about LGBT+ rights fell into the latter category. Her comprehension was good, and she could write coherently, but her nerves got the better of her at exam time, and she would invariably underperform.

Of course the kids who are talented, hard-working all-rounders and would have done well anyway will always be fine. And those who aren't that creative or articulate or analytical but who manage their time well may do better than they otherwise would have. But it's the kids who find academic work the hardest who will suffer the most. Support systems which had been built up over the years to allow them to at least access the paper were more or less removed in one fell swoop.

We're not talking here about wanting to dish out top grades to everyone – we're talking about giving everyone the best possible chance to achieve their potential. Not everyone is cut out for exams. Not being good at exams doesn't mean that you're inferior or even that you're not as good at the subject. And yet these reforms seem to perpetuate that belief. As usual, it's the weakest in society who suffer most, and it's all in the name of 'rigour'.

This latest change is part of a wider pattern that has been troubling me. For some time I have been asking myself whether I want to stay working in an education system where the priorities of Ofsted can trump the priorities of children, where exam results are treated as more important than character development or nurturing a love of learning or providing a well-rounded education in the broadest sense of the word, and where stress levels continue to ratchet up and up and up unchecked by school leaders or politicians or anyone else. There are still moments of real joy. But they are becoming fewer.

You Say Arse ...

Since joining the leadership team, I am teaching less and dealing with queries and complaints and problems more. You can bet your house that the moments which brighten my day, the times that remind me why I got into the job in the first place, are going to come in the lessons.

I have an engaged and enthusiastic, if not particularly academic, Year 13 class, and we're studying *The Wife of Bath's Tale* from Chaucer's *The Canterbury Tales* for A level English literature. I use the word 'we' very deliberately, because Middle English is located some distance outside my comfort zone when it comes to teaching. We are working through it together.

We have come to the bit where the Wife tells the story of Midas.

'Does anybody know anything about King Midas?' I ask optimistically.

'Wasn't he the one that everything he touched turned to gold?' one student responds.

'Brilliant!' I say. Another hand goes up.

'Didn't he also have the ears of an arse?' His words fall into a confused silence.

'Didn't he have the what?'

'I'm pretty sure he had an arse's ears.'

After a short pause I ask, 'Do you mean the ears of an ass?' For indeed, as I had learned from Google the night before, Midas had donkey's ears growing under his hair, which he was given by Apollo as a punishment for saying he thought someone else was a better musician than him.

The student seems to realise my confusion and laughs before explaining in his most helpful voice, 'No, sir, you might say "ass" because you're from up North. Down South we say "arse".'

Exclusion?

The student who was stabbed will make a full recovery; he sustained a fairly shallow leg wound. Much more complicated is how we deal with the perpetrator and how we respond as a school. The pupil who did it was on nobody's radar. He had not been in trouble before, either at school or with the police. He was a hard-working student. So what had possessed him to bring a knife into school and stab a fellow pupil?

The story that emerges is that the victim had been engaged in a playground game with some friends, including the attacker, when their competitiveness had got out of hand and developed into a physical fight. The boy who was stabbed was the initial aggressor. The boy who did the stabbing says that he was acting in self-defence.

This scenario prompts a lot of impassioned discussion at our leadership team meeting. The main debate is around whether the boy who did the stabbing should be permanently excluded from the school. Under normal circumstances, this would be a no-brainer, but the fact that he was himself the initial victim makes this more complicated. I am learning that, in reality, normal circumstances don't exist. There are always endless shades of grey and these decisions are difficult.

The uncertainty about what we should do is only increased when the perpetrator's father turns up at the school gates. He pleads with the member of staff who meets him to spare his son. He says that he is a good kid, and that the fate of any black boy who is permanently excluded from school is already sealed.

He's right, of course. Black pupils are disproportionately excluded from schools in the UK. In fact, studies have found that pupils of black Caribbean origin are three times more likely to be permanently excluded and more than twice as likely to be suspended as other pupils. And there is a close correlation between children who have been permanently excluded from school and knife crime among young people. The issues are complex and multifaceted, but the fact remains that young people who have been excluded from school are twice as likely to carry a knife as their peers.

And though the stats are shocking I can't say I find them massively surprising, because of what happens next to a child who has been excluded from school. If the child is lucky they might get a place at another school. In an ideal world they would then start afresh, put their misdeeds behind them and grasp the opportunity to make a success of their lives. I'm sure that happens sometimes. All I can say is that I haven't seen it often. These are frequently quite damaged young people, with complex social and emotional needs. They may have had tumultuous childhoods, or have seen or experienced things that children shouldn't see or experience. Because they're scared or insecure or traumatised or angry they can't always form normal relationships with their peers, and they feel their only option is to lash out, be it at teachers or their classmates or the system. That type of thing doesn't tend to go down too well in schools, so they're out again.

And if they don't get into another school, or when they've been thrown out of one or more, they often end up at the door of a Pupil Referral Unit. These are specialist schools that cater for pupils who can't handle mainstream education because of their extreme behaviour. I visited one once. The staff there unquestionably do God's work. They show inexhaustible patience in the face of the most extreme provocation imaginable. I remember walking down the corridor and hearing shouting coming from every direction. There was the sound of doors being rattled in their frames, and threats and swearing and howling. How would this man's son fare in an environment like that? What kind of future might he have there? What bad company might he fall into?

His dad also tells us more about why he thinks his boy was carrying the knife. He says that his son had been attacked several times in the preceding years just for walking through the wrong postcode. Gangs rule the streets, he says, and though his son isn't in one, that is no protection against attacks. He asks us what we would do if we were in that situation. Would we, hand on heart, say that we wouldn't be tempted to carry a weapon even after we had been attacked so many times?

We know that gangs are a real and present threat to our students, and we talk round and around about what the right thing to do is. In the end, we keep coming back to the fact that he brought a weapon into school and used it. We can't know if and when he would do that again, and we can't guarantee the safety of staff or students with him in the community. And we conclude that ultimately there needs to be a line in the sand: using a weapon in school has to be an offence which will get you excluded. And so, reluctantly, that's what we do. I don't know what happened to him in the longer term. But I think about him from time to time and hope that he was an exception to those statistics.

We also introduce random searches. The police bring in a 'knife arch', essentially a metal detector, and we collect classes from their lessons and escort them to the hall where they walk through it in turn. We think it works well as a deterrent. But what an environment for children, in the UK, in the twenty-first century, to go to school in.

A Success Story

One of the stars of the Year 13 group I am muddling through Chaucer with is called Chloe. She's the head girl of the school, and a dream to teach. She does extra research at home, she takes it upon herself to read other *Canterbury Tales*, she has something thoughtful to say in every discussion. And she somehow manages to do it all without coming across as holier-than-thou. She's popular and humble and affable.

Her other A level subjects are chemistry, biology and maths and she told me that her dream is to become a doctor. So when she arrives at the lesson one day beaming and announcing that she has been offered a place at medical school, the whole class celebrates with her. It's only at lunch-time in the staffroom, when I'm relaying the news to a colleague, that I learn about her background.

Chloe, it transpires, came to the school later than her peers and not speaking a word of English. She was a refugee from Liberia, and she had witnessed both her parents being murdered before she was even old enough to understand what the word 'murder' meant. She had been looked after in England by her older sisters, who dutifully came to parents' evenings and fulfilled the roles of both mum and dad.

If I'm honest, it is pretty rare to witness such a genuine success story in teaching. When you have a student who arrives with such a traumatic past, my experience is that it fails to work out well more often than it succeeds. They just stop coming to school, or they get into altercations or their circumstances change again and they have to move on. But Chloe is a bona-fide triumph for the school, for the wider community, and for society at large.

I've come in right at the very end of her school journey, but other staff have nurtured her from being a new arrival, unable to communicate at all, to someone who is on course to achieve top grades at A level. The local community have welcomed the family, and her peers elected her their leader. And she has got her education entirely for free, thanks to the British taxpayer. Naturally she has put the graft in, and nobody would claim that she had an easy ride. And now, all she wants to do is give back to the country that has supported her, by becoming a doctor. And she'll be a brilliant one. I know I am ludicrously soft, but as I see her getting ready to head to medical school I can't help but feel a little overcome at how much she deserves her success.

Visiting Zoe

While my mind has been occupied with parental complaints and rotas and data spreadsheets, Zoe has had news which makes all of that seem like inconsequential noise. Her cancer has returned. And this time it has spread to her lungs.

It is a small tumour she tells me, just millimetres long, and the doctors are optimistic that they'll be able to zap it so that it shrinks or, at worst, stays that size. Dan, she says, is looking after her better than she ever could have expected. But it means more chemotherapy blasting her body and more uncertainty and more agony for her and for Dan. We wander around Hampstead Heath chewing over life and death and love and family and pain and the fragility of health.

It's just a few weeks later that I get on a train to Cambridge to visit Zoe and Dan. I have heard from Dan that there has been a rapid and substantial decline in her condition. The cancer has moved from her lungs to her spine, causing the bones in her back to crumble, and she is in a lot of pain.

Dan meets me at the station and drives me to their home. He is positive and upbeat, but he tells me it has been tough. He doesn't say it, but I can tell from his voice, from his eyes and even from his posture that his love for Zoe is so deep that her pain causes him considerable pain.

Zoe is lying on the sofa when we walk in. She opens her eyes and smiles and her Northern warmth fills the room. Dan crouches beside her, puts his arm around her and gently, tenderly lifts her up. She looks like her old self. Her hair, or rather her wig, is perfectly arranged and her make-up is immaculate. As Dan fusses around finding the tablets and the medicine that Zoe needs to take, and sorts tea and coffee for us, Zoe shows me her Zimmer frame that she needs if she is to walk anywhere and she rolls her eyes. We laugh and I make a joke about how we always were old before our time, but there is nothing funny here.

What gets me most is that, in the same way Liz did in the corridor several years before, Zoe asks about me – what I've been up to, how work at the new school is going, how the colleagues compare. It all seems trivial.

It's not long before Zoe is visibly exhausted. I crouch down and hug her and her smile changes only briefly into a grimace as she adjusts her position on the sofa to return the hug. As Dan drives me back to the station he tells me how great an effort Zoe made that morning in order to appear well. Getting dressed is an enormous struggle. She got up early to ensure her wig looked perfect. She put make-up on for the first time in days.

On the train back to London I am left thinking about Zoe and Dan as a couple. Zoe's strength of spirit, her ability to maintain a sense of humour in the face of considerable suffering, and her capacity to think of others even when the focus should reasonably be on her, are genuinely remarkable.

And as for Dan ... I had always known that he was a brilliant teacher. He worked long into the evening thinking of ways to make his lessons more engaging, more lively, more likely to stretch the students in his class. He combined the hard work with an easy rapport and a brilliant sense of humour. But that day, on that visit, I realise that Dan is a hero. A man amongst men.

In looking after Zoe he shows the same meticulous attention to detail that he did in the classroom, the same passion and compassion, the same ability to laugh at himself and at ridiculous situations. He is gentle, loving and cheerful. As I watch him tend to her, he is the teacher and I sit at his feet.

Prayer Room

At our leadership team meeting we're looking at a letter which has been written to the head and signed by several Muslim students. In it they request a classroom which can be used as a place to pray by the school's Muslim community.

We are keen to oblige. It's a mature act on the students' behalf to write a letter, and it feels right that in an inclusive community they should have somewhere they can practise their faith. Somebody makes the point that students of any faith or none should be able to use the space for quiet reflection, so we decide to make it a multi-faith space.

We talk about which rooms might be suitable and practicalities like who will make sure it's opened for them and locked at the end of the session. And, naively, we don't think much more about it.

Hello, Stranger

I'm idly scrolling through my phone while waiting for a friend outside Holborn station in central London after work. Out of the corner of my eye I become aware of a figure hovering nearby. I presume he's one of London's many flyerers and I'm not really interested in hearing about the latest banging club night. He's standing oddly close to me and moving closer, and I can feel his gaze on me. I stare ever more intently on the phone. He's moving closer still.

He's extending his arm in my direction. And now he's speaking! 'Excuse me.' I can't believe he's engaging with me despite my sending every signal that I am not in the market for promotional material.

'Sorry to have bothered you,' he says. 'I just wanted to say that I really enjoyed your English lessons. I still read my copy of *Of Mice and Men* sometimes.' I turn around and look at him properly for the first time. It takes my mind a few moments to place the face. And then it's clearly Azad, who once thought that Margaret Thatcher had a torrid lesbian affair with Carol Ann Duffy.

He's grinning and I shake his hand and ask him how life's treating him. He's not a flyerer at all; he is temping in an office nearby, but saving money so he can go to college and study sports management. It's great to see him, and I reflect that I should revisit my policy on body language in the street.

Taking on the Regulator

As part of my ongoing managerial development, I find myself at a large training event where the morning's keynote speaker is Dame Glenys Stacey. She is the chief executive of Ofqual, the exams watchdog. My only real knowledge of Ofqual and what they do is that they defended the exam board that moved the grade boundaries for GCSE English in 2012, which resulted in all those children across the country getting a grade lower than they would have done the year before. The teaching unions took Ofqual to court over it, arguing it was grossly unfair and demanding that the grade boundaries be reviewed and students' grades moved up, but they lost.

And as she walks out onto the stage, with upbeat music playing and the audience clapping, all those feelings of resentment and injustice and anger come careering back. I remember the faces of the kids who opened their results envelopes with expectant eyes, believing they had done enough to get a C and finding out that they were close and yet not close enough. So I'm already feeling on edge as she begins her talk. And then she stands in front of a group of teachers, many of them English teachers who had been caught up in the 2012 debacle, and lectures us on the importance of fairness in the education system. I mean, for crying out loud. This is too much irony for me. Finally she stops speaking and she asks whether anyone has any questions.

I have a severe personality flaw. It was perhaps best described by my home economics teacher, Mrs Wilde, when I was about thirteen. She had given us back our summer exam papers which she had marked and gone through with us during the lesson. Based on what she had said I was convinced, rock-solid certain, that I should have had two more marks than I had been awarded. Other people, of a more normal disposition, would think, 'Ah well, it's only Year 9 home economics and it's only an internal exam. And we're only talking about a couple of per cent. And anyway, she's the expert and she knows what she's doing.'

Not me, sadly. I stood and argued my case for the whole of break time. I argued like I was a lawyer fighting for a client who had suffered the most major miscarriage of justice of the twentieth century. Which, in my eyes, I had. She gave me the extra marks, with hindsight just to make me go away, and I left feeling vindicated and not realising that I had made an idiot of myself. And I lacked the empathy to realise that I had just robbed the great Mrs Wilde of her break time. She later told my parents that she thought I had 'an over-heightened sense of justice'. She was right, but that was a kind way of putting it.

The same over-heightened sense of justice was well and truly triggered by Dame Glenys. That's why, as an out-of-body experience, I feel my hand going up when she asks whether anyone has any questions. My heart is thumping. I look around and see that dozens of hands are up and instantly start to relax a little as I see how unlikely it is that she will come to me. But then she is looking directly at me, and saying, 'Yes, the man in the blue shirt,' and my shirt is blue, and someone is handing me a microphone and before I know it my voice is booming around the hall.

'A lot of people in this room will find it quite hard to accept that you're talking to us about fairness today because what happened with GCSE English in 2012 was anything but fair, and you went to court to defend it. So my question is, "What would you say to my brilliant team of English teachers who worked their butts off for those kids, and whose morale you damaged by those actions, and what would you say to the young people who had the course of their lives altered by this injustice?"'

There is a sort of stunned silence. I think she was expecting questions more along the lines of, 'Could you tell us more about why fairness is important in education?' She eventually replies, 'Well, the first thing I would say is that I would very much like to come and visit your English team and have the opportunity to explain it to them myself ...' I don't really hear the rest of her answer because I'm lost in the horror of the realisation that Dame Glenys, the chief executive of Ofqual, is now apparently coming to my school.

She is as good as her word and a couple of months later addresses the team. She explains the process of setting grade boundaries and justifies why they had to be lower that year. Ultimately the court found that the correct procedure had been followed, but that doesn't mean that nothing unfair had happened.

Lots of children didn't get the grade that they, or their teachers, were expecting. They didn't get the grade that they would have received had they taken the exam any other year. And those grades will follow them, in many cases, for the rest of their lives.

Paul tells me that I am forbidden from provoking any other senior educational figures into visiting the school.

Multi-Faith Space

We are forced to return to our decision to open a multi-faith space rather sooner than planned. The newspapers in the last few days have been full of the story of three teenage girls from the same East London school who ran away to join the so-called Islamic State in Syria. It was a shocking case. These girls had been radicalised in the UK, and willingly left their homes to join an extremist military group believing that they would be part of something bigger, something divine, as well as following the promise of love and marriage. They stole jewellery from their families and sold it to fund their flights. They flew from Gatwick Airport near London to Istanbul in Turkey and more or less disappeared, immediately shielded by the shadowy cloak of a cruel and militant organisation.

How could we protect Muslim pupils worshipping in our multi-faith space from potential radicalisation? We have a very serious duty of care to them. The germ of fear was strengthened when a member of the leadership team popped his head around the door, and didn't find pupils on prayer mats, but rather one student addressing all the others in Arabic and reading from the Qur'an. The chances are that this was entirely devotional, but there is enough doubt for us to lay down a few new ground rules. We draw up a rota to ensure that a senior member of staff will be in the room at lunchtime every day to monitor proceedings. All conversations will have to be conducted in English. And if any of the group leaders refuse to agree to these rules we will have to re-evaluate whether we are able to provide such a space.

It seems like the best available way to respect the students' desire to have a space for prayer, whilst also ensuring that sufficient safeguards are in place to protect their well-being. But it is a policy which will come under national scrutiny.

At Any Time

I am responding to another complaint: a parent feels that their child is much brighter than any of us have realised, or than any of their work hitherto has suggested, and is asking that we push her more enthusiastically. I compose an email response which assures the parent that we will do everything we can to uncover these depths that have remained so stubbornly hidden up until now. I reread it to check that it makes my point but with a tone that isn't too sarcastic or dismissive and add a quick sign-off before hitting send.

After I confidently dispatch the message I happen to cast my eye over it again. I once read somewhere that there is a law of the universe known as 'Muphry's law'. It's a deliberate misspelling of Murphy's law and it states that you will spot a typo a few milliseconds after you have hit print or send. Instead of the friendly and approachable 'Please do not hesitate to contact me at any time,' I have written the sub-optimal, 'Please do not contact me at any time.' Night or day, I couldn't care less.

It is only rivalled by the time I had to email the terrifying female deputy head and opened with the unfortunate line, 'I know you're really busty but ...'

Syria

A message goes around that the leadership team are to attend an emergency meeting first thing on Monday morning. As we huddle around the table, Paul explains the facts as best he knows them. Over the weekend three male teenagers, two cousins aged seventeen and another nineteen-year-old, were stopped in an airport in Istanbul. They had apparently been planning to travel onwards to Syria to join IS. One of the younger boys was an A level student at our school. There is an audible gasp when Paul says his name: a straight-A student with aspirations to go to a top university.

The boys had been intercepted and were safe and on their way back to the UK. Paul said that there had been some press interest already, and that there was likely to be more. He wasn't wrong. It starts with a local journalist turning up at the school door, and over the course of the morning there are national journalists from most of the major papers. By lunchtime this crowd have been joined by TV crews and reporters who broadcast live from outside the gates. We are told that we should all don our fetching hi-vis jackets at the end of the school day and patrol at the front of the building, trying to stop any parents or students from talking to journalists.

Clearly it's a serious situation, but there is also something vaguely ridiculous about ten men and women in bright jackets running up and down trying to place their bodies between journalists and children. It's like a cross between a game of Pac-Man and a Benny Hill sketch. It's ultimately futile too. It's not possible to stop people talking to the press outside the gate and even if it were, they can obviously talk to the press in literally any other location.

And hardened hacks aren't, it turns out, put off the scent by a few luminescent teachers. We hear the next day that some tabloid journalists spent the night outside the home of the student from our school who travelled, posting notes through the letterbox to his traumatised family, with promises of money in return for an interview.

The next day the *Independent* proclaims, 'School attended by returned would-be Isis teen enforced Friday prayers in English ... the new rules, including having a teacher present during the prayers, were brought in three weeks ago.' Other papers have similar write-ups, all of which seem to imply that the school had only recently 'cracked down' on an apparent scourge of radicalisation. They hinted, without ever actually saying it, that the grooming must have taken place in school. In fact it had not happened in school, nor at the student's mosque, but through an older friend unconnected to either. We had been proactive in taking steps to protect pupils, but you wouldn't have gathered that from reading the papers.

It's all a salutary lesson on what it's like to be embroiled in a press storm, as well as the power of dangerous ideologies to convince even the most apparently well-adjusted of students. School staff meet the boy's family and agree that it's probably best for him if he doesn't come back to our school where he would have inevitable notoriety, but that he should start his A levels again elsewhere, after completing a de-radicalisation programme. His name was kept out of the press, so a fresh start is at least possible.

I chalk it all up as another thing we weren't taught on our PGCE course.

Budget

The senior leadership team are gathered together, poring over a series of spreadsheets which seem to cover the entire table: the school's budget. The eye-watering news the business manager has just delivered is that in the next academic year we will have £2 million less than we have had this year. The government has reviewed the funding formula it uses to allocate money to schools. Where once inner-city London schools lagged behind others in terms of results, and were the priority for enhanced funding, now they are seen as a success story, so the money is going away again. The funding allocated per pupil has been significantly reduced, and the sixth form has been particularly badly hit. Add into the mix a growing number of pupils at the school, and the effect of the lost funding is amplified.

We start going through the school's expenditure line by line, looking for anything that can reasonably be cut. Photocopying budgets are first in the firing line. Someone suggests that all pupils could be expected to share handouts one between two and heads of department will have to ration the amount of photocopying that each teacher in their team does. The savings have begun. Teachers receive a small payment of £7 per lunch duty as they're not part of teachers' contracted hours. The senior team agree that we will waive that fee and just do them from goodwill.

Next for the chop are the taxis and free breakfasts the school provides to make sure the most vulnerable students from the most chaotic homes get to school on time and have some food before lessons start. Then it's the small group tuition in English and maths for the weakest students. And so it goes on. Each cut feels genuinely painful. We are dismantling the safety net that has been built up over the years to help the poorest and the most in need, to make sure that kids are kept in the system and supported. To help students like Kieron who, through no fault of their own, have had tough lives and need more of a helping hand. It's the safety net that caught Chloe, and ensured she went from vulnerable child to trainee doctor. It works. And it's being hacked away.

The mood in the room couldn't be more despondent. We feel that we have gone as far as we can and further than we should. We tally up the savings we have made. It's not even £200,000. Barely a tenth of the savings we need to make.

So we go through line by line again, this time pausing to consider things we had thought utterly untouchable the first time around. The school counsellor, a lifeline to countless children and more than a few staff, will have her hours cut. A few years before, the school had established a special inclusion centre for kids who weren't able to stay in mainstream lessons because of poor behaviour. Pupils could be sent there to continue with their work, but they would also receive targeted small-group support from highly experienced special needs teachers. The beauty of that system is that these pupils would otherwise be officially excluded from school. And once they're excluded, the chances of them dropping out of the system altogether rise dramatically. With no one outside their family looking out for them, they're more likely to end up with no qualifications and the stats show they're more likely to fall into crime. The unit works minor miracles every day. And yet it has to go, as the teachers working there must be redeployed to teach in the main school.

Then there is staffing. The first red line when we started off was the desire to avoid redundancies. But we look at every class across the school and start culling. Where previously there were fourteen maths classes in Years 10 and 11, next year there will be twelve. Classes will be bigger which isn't good for students. But it will mean less human resource is needed. So it continues across the departments. We agree that we won't replace any teaching staff who leave over the next few months unless absolutely necessary.

But that creates its own complications. I am responsible for producing the school staffing plan and timetable. When I sit down to write next year's, I am told to do so anticipating having seven fewer teachers than the year before. The geography department is understaffed due to teachers not being replaced. But the maths department is overstaffed as no one has left and they've had their classes reduced. So there's nothing else for it – some maths teachers are going to have to teach geography. We have music teachers teaching languages and art teachers teaching history and all manner of odd ways of plugging the gaps. The result is that kids are taught by people who aren't specialists in the subject, who don't want to be there, and who in many cases don't know much more about the subject than the kids they are teaching.

The news is no better in the sixth form. We calculate that class sizes need to be as high as seventeen to make them financially viable. We decide on a general principle that we will not routinely run classes with fewer than fifteen students. But that puts whole subjects at risk. With our school's student profile, science and maths and economics and business studies will always be oversubscribed. But art and graphics and music and drama and performing arts and design technology and French and Spanish and German are all massively under threat.

As we reach the end of our marathon cost-cutting exercise, the amount we are saving is starting to get near where it needs to be. But it's a massacre. Ring fences lie in ruins and red lines are distant memories. When we tell the staff, naturally they are angry with us, because their working conditions will be worse. And because their already difficult jobs, which they are working flat out to do to the best of their ability, will be harder still. And they're angry on behalf of the kids. Of course they are. And rightly so.

But, I want to tell them, I am just as angry. No part of me wanted anything to do with this. But what choice did we have? We don't decide how much money our school is going to be allocated. I head home feeling deflated and grubby, disillusioned and defeated.

On the news that evening an Education Minister is asked about schools that are struggling for funding. 'The education budget is ring-fenced and we have not cut even a penny from the money that goes directly to schools.' His words could not have riled me more. While technically true about the overall spend, he conveniently omits the fact that the number of children on the school roll is going up, so keeping the funding the same is a real-terms cut. He ignores inflation, so that's another real terms cut. Then there's the new funding formula that means some schools, like ours, will receive a smaller slice of the pie. And he doesn't mention the fact that the government has required schools to stump up a significantly higher share of employees' pension contributions than they have done in the past, without any extra funding to do that. Another real-terms cut. But anybody watching the politician might perfectly reasonably think, 'Oh well, if the government is protecting funding, then it must be the fault of schools mismanaging their finances.'

It's the worst kind of leadership. They create a problem and then deftly pass it on to the men and women on the front line and absolve themselves of all responsibility. I am nearly crying with rage.

The fact that funding is going down at the same time that accountability is going up almost exponentially is a toxic combination. That the government deny all responsibility is, for me, the final straw. The job of the Education Secretary should involve supporting teachers and ensuring that they are equipped to do the job, not pushing and prodding them to achieve more with less and berating them publicly when that proves difficult. Schools are becoming pressure cookers to the point where everyone working there, almost all of them diligent and dedicated to the cause, thinks that they might face the chop at any moment.

It all feels a very long way from the wide-eyed enthusiasm of the kid who was so excited to get the blackboard for his eighth birthday. Something is going to have to give.

Joy And Sadness

There is, however, a perfect antidote for my growing sense of gloom at work. My little brother is getting married. Inexplicably he has found a girl who is clever and funny, beautiful and kind, and she even seems to quite like him. When he asked me to be his best man I cried, much to both of our embarrassment, and as I sit in the hotel going over my speech for the next day one more time, and checking that the rings are definitely in my suit pocket, there's emotion very close to the surface.

My phone has been going all evening as various family and friends coordinate their arrivals and make plans to meet up. So when it rings again, I assume it'll be someone else who has got lost on the windy roads surrounding the venue and wants me to somehow guide them here. But instead I hear the voice of one of my former colleagues in Essex. From the pauses, from the intonation, from the quiet apologies, something in me knows instantly what's coming. She tells me she has just spoken to Dan and that Zoe has left us. Dan said it was peaceful, and she looked relieved.

How do you describe those moments when time stops, all noise and bustle around you is suddenly muted and your mind spins and you feel sick and confused and numb? They say your life flashes before your eyes just before you die. I see Zoe's life flash before mine, or at least the decade I shared with her. How she stood up for Northerners in our first conversation. Her poking her toe at the flat tyre. Her telling me off for wearing trousers and shirts which didn't match. Having lunch with her in the swanky restaurant. The champagne. Her sending me a note to tell me she was bored during Year 8 assessments. Her interest in everyone, and her ability to draw the best out of people, adults as much as children. How beautiful she looked on her wedding day. Her laugh. And Dan. The great love they shared. The way he made her laugh through the pain. How he nursed her and cherished her and held her.

I lie in my hotel bed, these memories of Zoe spinning around. Sleep comes at some point, and the sun rises as usual. And there's no option but to celebrate the wedding, and give the speech and dance in the ceilidh and block it out. The wedding is full of hope and exuberance and love, but every time I remember, it hits me afresh. Life's greatest joy and greatest pain existing side by side in one day.

Tunisia

It's a couple of weeks later. Life, of course, goes on, but as my brother embarks on married life, my thoughts keep returning to Zoe and Dan and how tragically short their marriage was.

They are on my mind as I sit in a leadership team meeting. We get to an item on the agenda labelled 'Tunisia terror attacks'. A few days ago, a terrorist inspired by Islamic State killed thirty-eight people, thirty of them Britons, on a beach near Sousse in Tunisia. They were just people lounging around, enjoying their holiday. A twenty-four-year-old beauty blogger who had recently got engaged to her childhood sweetheart. A forty-nine-year-old man who was shot and killed alongside his father and nineteen-year-old nephew. A fifty-nine-year-old man who died heroically shielding his wife from the gunfire.

It's the randomness of the whole thing I find so moving. Ordinary people who got up that day, had their buffet breakfast, wondered what to do next and decided to head to the beach, not knowing the violent end that awaited them. It's yet another reminder of our mortality and the importance of making the most of life.

The UK government has announced that there will be a national minute's silence to remember the victims. It is to take place at noon on Friday and we are discussing whether the school should participate. I share a little of how upsetting I have found it all, and say that I'm firmly of the opinion that we should mark it. A senior colleague responds that he agrees, saying, 'Ofsted love to see kids taking part in civic activities.'

It's a comment that causes me to do a double-take. Our school, like many others, is already in Ofsted's grip on so many issues. So much of the work that we slave over is done, not for the benefit of any child, but so that we can present it to some inspectors to keep them happy and let them tick the relevant boxes. I feel as though our ability to provide great teaching for our students has already been compromised by the need to constantly prove our excellence on paper.

But now we're saying that the reason we would hold a minute's silence is not to honour the victims of a brutal terrorist attack, but so that we might impress those same bureaucrats? That is about as far as it's possible to be from why I went into teaching. The comment sticks with me over the following days. It seems to epitomise the whole problem with our education system and its misplaced priorities. But the remark is a symptom, not a cause. I don't particularly blame the guy who said it. He's just allowed the external pressures to get into his head, and he's lost focus on what's important. But the more I dwell on the comment, the more troubling I find it. And I'm also worried that, if I stay in the role for much longer, I'm in danger of getting sucked into that corrosive way of thinking.

In Memoriam

The school in Essex is to hold a memorial service for Zoe. Dan has asked me to say a few words about her, so I am reliving our stories yet again in an attempt to put into words how vivacious and fun and loving she was.

I dig out a letter that Zoe gave me on my last day at that school, several years before. She pressed it into my hand as I walked out the door for the last time. It's written on beautiful notepaper, and her handwriting is immaculate. It's Zoe all over.

Dear Ryan,

I wanted you to know how profound an impact you have had upon me and my career. I thought the other day what path I would have taken had it not been for you, and I am so grateful for all your guidance and support. It has been truly invaluable.

Many people at this school have experienced your professional gifts, but there aren't many who can say you helped them through cancer treatment. I still remember telling you my fears that day in the store cupboard, and you showed your positive, 'can-do' attitude at its finest. I can't express how much I will value that for the rest of my life.

My true friend, I will miss seeing you in September, but please keep in touch. Here are some of the reasons you should:

1) *The day we got lost on the way to school.*

2) *The fateful day we tried to fill your tyres with air.*

3) *Me falling in the corridor on our first day.*

4) *The day you squirted water at a child with Down Syndrome.*

5) *Your love of Tom Baker jumpers.**

*This last point needs a little explanation. It wasn't long into our friendship that Zoe became so exasperated at my fashion sense that she insisted we spend a Saturday afternoon buying me a new wardrobe. My fundamental shopping technique is to spend as little time as possible in any shops. It turned out Zoe had the almost exact opposite philosophy. She had made an itinerary of shops we would visit, and I had not darkened the door of many of them before. Ted Baker was one such establishment. As the afternoon wore on I asked whether we might consider slimming down our plans; maybe we could cross Tom Baker off the list? Apparently this 'summed up the enormity of the task' Zoe faced.

The letter ends:

Finally, I hope you know that you have earned my total REPSECT.

All my love, always,

Zoe

The letter brilliantly encapsulates Zoe's voice, her humour, warmth and sincerity. I regret not offering more support throughout her treatment, being caught up in the busyness of day-to-day life when I should have devoted more time to being helpful. But she was all about making other people feel good about themselves. It captures her to a T, and each of the five stories she mentions goes straight into my address for her memorial service.

The day itself is really special. Teachers take to the stage to describe how Zoe was a dream colleague. Current students speak about their love for her lessons, and former students describe how she changed the direction of their lives. Dan's eulogy is moving and heartfelt and transcendent. Having read from *Les Misérables* at their wedding, at Dan's request I read from F. Scott Fitzgerald's *The Great Gatsby* at her memorial service. It's a book Zoe had taught and loved. Fitzgerald is describing Jay Gatsby, but everyone in the room is thinking only of Zoe:

[It was] one of those rare smiles with a quality of eternal reassurance in it, that you may come across four or five times in life. It faced – or seemed to face – the whole external world for an instant, and then concentrated on you with an irresistible prejudice in your favour. It understood you just so far as you wanted to be understood, believed in you as you would like to believe in yourself and assured you that it had precisely the impression of you that, at your best, you hoped to convey.

For many of us at Zoe's memorial service, this was the second time in just a few years that we'd had to sit in this hall and say farewell to a superb teacher and human lost far too soon. The value of our health and the suddenness with which it can all be taken away was at the forefront of my mind.

Those circumstances, and the double reminder that life is short, are enough to convince me to finally write my resignation. The highs in teaching are incomparable but, today, the costs to teachers are so great. After ten years at the front of the classroom I have applied to go back to university and study for a master's in broadcast journalism. The other great love of the kid who enjoyed marking was radio, and I hope I haven't left it too late to have a crack at a second career.

In some ways the two roles are similar, I write in my application. They both involve taking complex, messy situations and trying to present them in a way which is clear and easily understandable to an audience which is at best passive, and at worst, actively disengaged.

I leave teaching burned out and frustrated with all the nonsense. Something is clearly wrong. Two in five teachers quit the profession within five years of qualifying; 80 per cent report high stress levels in their job. The bureaucracy, accountability and absurd pressure on teachers to tick boxes can be crippling.

For all the issues, I hope this goodbye isn't for ever. If things improved, I would be at the front of the queue to return, because it's important to distinguish all the noise from the absolute pleasure of being in the classroom. At its root, that elemental and ancient process of passing on knowledge and skills to the next generation is the best job you will find. Working with young people, in all their unpredictability and forthrightness and hilarity, is naturally sometimes frustrating, but overwhelmingly it's incredible fun.

On the off chance that an Education Secretary ever reads this, here are a few friendly words of advice: we must fund schools adequately; give teachers the status and standing they deserve, including paying them properly; look beyond exam results to the development of the whole child; and trust teachers to get on with their jobs. Are there bad teachers out there? Of course. That's the nature of any workplace. And they should be supported so they can improve and weeded out if they can't or won't. But in my experience they are few and far between. It doesn't make sense to focus so much time and resource on checking up obsessively on them.

We could channel all that surveillance energy into looking for ways to support teachers. I'm not talking about bonuses or holidays or anything extravagant. I'm talking about making sure that schools have enough money to give teachers the tools they need to do their work properly, creating a credible plan to retain teachers in the job, and speaking up for the profession publicly.

Talk to teachers, listen to their concerns and involve them in planning future strategy. We might just stop great people leaving the profession; who knows how many potential scientists or writers or linguists or artists will miss their vocation in life because the teacher who would have inspired them to follow their dreams was one of the thousands who walked away?

If you're a teacher, I salute you. You will almost certainly have had your fill of people who think that you clock off for the day at three. You'll have met with Triumph and Disaster, not just once, but multiple times a day in the classroom, and you'll have kept going in spite of both. You'll have cajoled and encouraged and berated and corrected and picked up and comforted and advised and congratulated more students than you can remember, but they will remember you.

There is a role for all of us too, whether or not we work in schools, whether or not we have children of school age. A healthy, productive, thriving education system is in all of our interests. We can take an interest in education policy at election time and do what we can to put our schools front and centre in politics. And many schools are crying out for governors to sit on their boards. They need switched-on, engaged people who can hold the leadership to account but do so with rational heads and a sense of perspective.

If you have a teacher amongst your loved ones, you might well have been frustrated at the time they have to give to the job long outside working hours, the stress it causes them and perhaps the way that their teacher persona sometimes bleeds into their personal life. But there's quite a high probability they're a hero, fighting every day against a system which seems intent on making their jobs as difficult as possible. Get them a drink.

Acknowledgements

I have heard that it takes a village to raise a child, but I had no idea that it takes a small army to create a book. First in the battalion is Greg Clowes who, on a long train journey north, suggested that my ramblings could, with a bit of work, come together into a book. For your belief in *Let That Be a Lesson*, your encouragement and your wisdom, I am extremely grateful.

Lots of friends read various drafts and offered sage words: a huge and heartfelt thank you to Peter Cardwell, John McIntosh, Hannah Middleton, Jen Whyntie, Chris Mattley and Phil Jones. A finer collection of minds, critics and encouragers a man couldn't ask for.

Versions of some of the chapters started out life as articles written for the *Guardian*'s Teacher Network. Kate Hodge, then editor of those pages, took me under her wing as I nervously dipped my toe in the world of educational writing: thank you, Kate, for trusting me.

When I googled 'literary agent' one afternoon, not even really knowing what an agent was, up popped the smiling face of Caroline Hardman at Hardman & Swainson. Over a coffee in Somerset House she patiently explained how to get a book published, and she was there at every step of the process with her trademark no-nonsense advice.

The team at Chatto & Windus have shown me the same patience, care and dedication that they have shown my manuscript. Charlotte Humphery, my editor, is simply exceptional;

generous in words and time, insightful beyond what is reasonable for any human being, and a joy to work with.

From the moment I put fingers to keyboard, I was acutely, painfully aware that I was telling other people's stories as well as my own. That is particularly true with Liz and Zoe, so I am beyond grateful to their loved ones who were gracious enough to trust me to pay my tributes in this book. They were the best of us. I only hope that I have communicated half of how remarkable they were, and how much I thought of them. They live on in the lives of those they taught and inspired.

I must, of course, thank my mum and dad, Peter and Sheena, who are the absolute best examples of the genre and two of the best people I have ever met, as well as Jamie, Becca, Orla, Ted, Sal and Ian. Ed and Atticus: you are both just brilliant; thank you for supporting me.

I would be remiss not to thank my own teachers, without whom I definitely wouldn't have gone into teaching. The staff of Friends' School in Lisburn and Dalriada School in Ballymoney were, and still are, superb.

And lastly thanks to all the outstanding colleagues I had over the years at two great schools. The head teachers and my line managers at both were excellent at cutting through the nonsense to the extent that it's possible to do so. Thanks as well to all the kids who passed through my classroom. Even when it felt like our governmental overlords were trying to squeeze every drop of fun from the job, you (almost) always brought the joy. If I ever told you off, I'd like you to know that, whatever I said, I meant every word of it.